ANOTHER WORLD LIES BEYOND

ANOTHER WORLD LIES BEYOND

Creating Liu Fang Yuan,
      the Huntington's Chinese Garden

Edited by T. June Li

Huntington Library · San Marino, California

This book is one of a series of publications on the Huntington
Botanical Gardens made possible by a generous contribution
from Peter and Helen Bing.

Copy and Production Editing by Han-yun Chang,
Susan Green, and Jean Patterson
Design by Picnic Design
Principal photography by John Sullivan, supplemented by
Don Alschuler, Lisa Blackburn, Jim Folsom, Laurie Sowd,
Lu Hongren, ValleyCrest Landscape Co., and Vivian Zhu.
Historical photographs are from the Huntington's collections.
Illustrations by Lisa Pompelli and He Xiaojian
Index by Jean Patterson
Prepress by Charles Allen Imaging Experts
Printed in South Korea

Front and back cover photography by John Sullivan

Library of Congress Cataloging in Publication Data

Another world lies beyond : creating Liu Fang Yuan, the
Huntington's Chinese garden / edited by T. June Li.
        p. cm.
        Includes bibliographical references and index.
        ISBN 978-0-87328-175-1 (alk. paper)
1. Gardens, Chinese—California—Design. I. Li, T. June. II. Title:
Creating Liu Fang Yuan, the Huntington's Chinese garden.
SB457.55.A56 2008
712.09794'93—dc22
                2008023791

CONTENTS

8   Acknowledgments   Steven Koblik

11   The Huntington Collections and the Chinese Community
       Peter J. Blodgett and Robert C. Ritchie

15   Foreword   Wan-go H. C. Weng

Section 1   **Liu Fang Yuan, the Chinese Garden at the Huntington**

19   Liu Fang Yuan, the Chinese Garden at the Huntington
       T. June Li

29   The Making of Liu Fang Yuan: A Brief History
       Laurie Sowd

Section 2   **Names of the Structures and Sites—Poetic Inspirations**

43   The Necessity of Names in Chinese Gardens
       Richard E. Strassberg

53   The Implied Visitor: Names and Their Meanings in
       Liu Fang Yuan   Yang Ye

63   Decoration and Themes in Liu Fang Yuan   T. June Li

Section 3   **A Botanical Overview**

75   Chinese Plants and Liu Fang Yuan:
       A Botanical Heritage   James Folsom

87   A Garden Glossary for Liu Fang Yuan

102   Map

105   Appendix A: Names in Liu Fang Yuan

113   Appendix B: Wood Materials in the Garden Structures

114   Appendix C: Poets, Calligraphers, and Artists

116   Selected Bibliography

120   Index

126   Editor's Acknowledgments

ACKNOWLEDGMENTS

T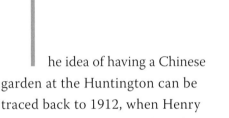he idea of having a Chinese garden at the Huntington can be traced back to 1912, when Henry Edwards Huntington purchased a Japanese house and an arch bridge, and created what was understood to be an "Oriental garden" in an arroyo west of his home. Huntington knew little—if anything—about the very different landscape traditions among Asian cultures; his garden was a bit of an amalgam. Over time, more Japanese features were added and, as a result, the garden became distinctly Japanese. Much later, with the help of Jim Folsom, Marge and Sherm Telleen Director of the Botanical Gardens, we began envisioning a Chinese garden, to help visitors understand the very rich and important distinctions in Asian garden traditions. The great Chinese garden landscape in fact came first among these traditions—it is, in many respects, the precursor to all gardens. Moreover, botanical science tells us that, like so much of the plant life in North America, the majority of the plants at the Huntington originated in China. So it was no surprise that, given the opportunity to envision a new garden, Jim, along with Huntington staff and friends, began to dream about a Chinese garden at the Huntington.

The Gardens Overseer Committee, with the support of some initial gifts, commissioned Chinese garden historian and designer Frances Tsu to produce preliminary designs for a new Chinese garden. These drawings were very influential in both scope and character as the Gardens Committee continued its conversations about the nature and desirability of such a garden. One member of the Gardens Overseer Committee, Peter Paanakker, was particularly impressed, and in 2000 launched the project by leaving the Huntington a bequest of $10 million to construct a Chinese garden. This remarkable lead gift provided the impetus to move the dream to reality. The Huntington Board of Trustees allocated half of the Paanakker gift to construction, with the other half reserved to endow the garden's operation. Jim Folsom took responsibility for initiating the project, with the help of Laurie Sowd, Associate Vice President for Operations. Another designer, Jin Chen, who was trained in both China and the United States, was hired to design the garden and help oversee construction.

Chen's leadership proved critical to the success of the project, culminating in the adoption of a clear set of principles: Chinese firms would produce the garden's design and building materials in China; the garden would follow the best traditions of Chinese garden construction; and the project would be a bicultural effort from start to finish. Working from Chen's extensive and complex master plan, the Huntington opted to construct phase one, a beautiful Chinese garden with seven pavilions, five bridges, and a lake with all its infrastructure. Everything, from sculptural rocks to carefully kiln-fired roof tiles, would come from China. These would then be shipped to San Marino and assembled here—no small feat, given the special challenges of building an authentic Chinese garden in seismically active Southern California. Laurie Sowd's essay in this volume traces the process of constructing the garden to meet California's building codes. It was a unique effort, both for our stateside team—Jim Fry and ValleyCrest Landscape Development Company—and our Chinese partners—the Suzhou Institute of Landscape Architecture Design and its construction team.

Costs more than doubled from the original estimates because of the complexity of the project, but efforts to raise the necessary funds met with great success. Major foundations stepped forward, including the Starr Foundation, the James Irvine Foundation, the Avery-Tsui Foundation, and Wallis Annenberg and the Annenberg Foundation. Corporations such as East West Bank, Cathay Bank, Air China, and COSCO–China Ocean Shipping (Group) Company made gifts in cash and in kind. A group of generous individuals, primarily from the diverse Chinese communities of California and abroad, provided exceptional advice and support, sharing financial resources as well as time and talent. A common purpose has inspired us all: to appreciate and understand Chinese culture through the lens of the Chinese Garden.

June Li, curator of the Chinese Garden since 2004, has provided invaluable expertise and leadership. She led the American and Chinese teams through a series of conversations that gave substance to their bicultural efforts, and she provided design perspectives and programmatic enhancements that have enriched the Huntington's efforts to establish a center for Chinese culture.

Liu Fang Yuan, the Garden of Flowing Fragrance, is a living place that will continue to evolve. I invite you to enjoy its beauty, its tranquility, and its celebration of human endeavor and achievement.

Steven Koblik
President, The Huntington Library, Art Galleries, and Botanical Gardens

John David Borthwick (Scottish, 1825–1900), "Chinese Camp in the Mines," *Three Years in California* (Edinburgh, 1857). RB 257, Huntington Library.

Joseph Warren Revere (American, 1812–1880), "Street in San Francisco," 1849. Watercolor drawing from his manuscript autobiography. HM 56913, Huntington Library.

THE HUNTINGTON COLLECTIONS
and the CHINESE COMMUNITY

In 1919, when Henry Edwards Huntington established the institution that bears his name, he envisioned not merely a private storehouse of personal treasures but a great library that would support advanced scholarly research and the dissemination of knowledge through publications, conferences, lectures, and seminars. To realize his vision, Huntington committed himself to purchasing entire libraries and large groups of personal papers, even when the contents seemed rather mundane. That search for comprehensiveness has continued to characterize the Library's acquisitions policy. Generations of librarians have cast the net ever wider, accumulating letters, diaries, guidebooks, travel narratives, photographs, drawings, and other rare materials that document the encounters of peoples and cultures across the North American continent over the last five centuries.

One such encounter unfolded in the wake of the 1848 discovery of gold in California, as growing numbers of immigrants from China crossed the Pacific Ocean on a journey to a place they described as "Gold Mountain." The Huntington's vast holdings related to the California Gold Rush include letters, diaries, drawings, and lithographs that depict the arrival of these sojourners in the 1850s, the increasingly prominent role they played in California's economic development, and the mounting hostility with which Euro-Americans regarded them. The Library holds numerous examples of the voluminous pamphlet literature that began to appear in

Y. C. Hong in front of his office in Chinatown.

the 1850s and continued for decades, condemning or praising the impact of Chinese immigration on California's economy, politics, and social conditions —even after the passage of the Chinese Exclusion Act of 1882. Other collections containing photographs, labor accounts, local tax rolls, and travel diaries capture glimpses of the many contributions of Chinese labor and entrepreneurship to the development of California, from the farms and ranches of the Central Valley to the urban "China towns" in which so many Chinese immigrants came to reside.

This story can be followed into the twentieth century through records from the Pacific Mail Steamship Company and other sources, which include information about Chinese immigration and the employment of Chinese workers in the maritime trades. The papers of Y. C. Hong, a prominent Chinese-American immigration lawyer in downtown Los Angeles, illuminate both the workings of the immigration process and aspects of Hong's own career from the 1920s through to the 1950s. Various political and legal collections in the Library detail the difficult struggle of Chinese-Americans against discrimination of all kinds, as they worked to establish their rights under such cardinal principles as equal protection under the law.

The Chinese community whose history is recorded by the Huntington's collections has continued to expand and evolve, just as the Chinese population in Los Angeles itself has boomed, following the revision of the federal immigration quotas in 1965. Today, new immigrants bring with them a global viewpoint, both economically and culturally, that in turn fully engages and enhances the global perspectives of this region's economy and culture. In time, the Huntington will collect the papers and preserve the history of these individuals and families as well.

Liu Fang Yuan, the Garden of Flowing Fragrance, will be the basis of international conferences and lectures on the history and meaning of gardens in Chinese culture. These programs will further enhance understanding of the richness and distinctiveness of Chinese art, literature, and history.

Peter J. Blodgett
H. Russell Smith Foundation Curator, Western American Manuscripts

Robert C. Ritchie
W. M. Keck Foundation Director of Research and Education

ARTICLES OF AGREEMENT made, entered into and concluded this *28th* day of *July*, in the Year of Our Lord, One thousand Eight hundred and *Forty nine* Between *Jacob P. Leese Esq of Monterey* - of the one part and *Ai chinaman* of the other part, Witness that for the consideration hereinafter contained on the part of the said *Jacob P. Leese Esq* he the said *Ai* doth hereby covenant, promise and agree with, and to the said *Jacob P. Leese Esq* that he the said *Ai* will proceed in and on board of a certain *Brig* or Vessel called the *Eveline* whereof *Cooper* is Master now lying in the Harbour of Hongkong, and about to proceed on a voyage to *San Francisco* Port or Ports, on the West Coast of America, and that he will any where in that Country, for the space or period of **(3)** *three* Years from the date of his arrival at the Port of destination, work as *a Tailor* or otherwise to the best of his knowledge and ability, under the orders and directions, of the said *Jacob P Leese Esq* or any other person holding this Contract. And that he the said *Ai* will keep and provide himself with all the necessary, and proper tools of his trade, and will also find, and provide his own clothing. And that he will not do or assist to do or direct or aid in any manner whatsoever any work or business, other than, that ordered or directed by the said *Jacob P. Leese Esq* or any other persons to whom this contract may be transferred. And these presents further witness that in consideration of the covenants herein before contained on the part of the said *Ai*

he the said *Jacob P. Leese Esq* doth hereby for himself his Heirs Executors, and Administrators covenant promise, and agree with, and to the said *Ai* that he his Survivors or Substitutes shall and will afford to him a passage in the above mentioned Vessel, to the West Coast of America, and shall, and will as soon as he shall have entered upon such work or trade of *a Tailor* as aforesaid furnish and provide him with lodgings, and suitable provisions, and food for, and during the said space or period of **(3)** *three* Years, and that the said *Ai* is to be paid for his work at the rate of **(#15)** *Fifteen* Dollars per month payable monthly in the due, and proper fulfilment, and completion of their said agreement, and covenants herein before contained, the said wages to be computed for the period of **(3)** *three* Years from the date the said *Ai* shall arrive at the Port of destination. And it is hereby agreed by and between the said parties hereto that the said *Ai* shall not receive any wages until, and after the Sum of *Thirty* **(30)** Dollars advanced to the said *Ai* shall have been paid off, and satisfied, and the said *Ai* doth hereby acknowledge the receipt of the said advance so made to him by the said *Jacob P Leese Esq* And it is hereby further agreed, that in case the said *Jacob P. Leese Esq* or his substitute *not requiring* the services of the said *Ai* at any time during the said period of **(3)** *three* Years he the said *Jacob P Leese Esq* or his substitute shall be at liberty to cancell this Contract on giving to said *Ai* One Month's notice, and from and after the expiration of such one Month's notice, this contract shall be null and void.

In Witness whereof the said parties to the presents have hereunto set their Hands and affixed their Seals at Victoria, Hongkong aforesaid the Day and Year first before written.

Signed Sealed and delivered after being
first duly explained in the presence of *A Shue* 書

W Brinley

Henry Anthon Jr
acting Vice Consul
United States of America

覃北喜云

`Ai`

J P Leese

Jacob P. Leese, labor contract with Ai, Chinaman, Hong Kong, July 28, 1849. Mariano Vallejo collection, VA 160, Huntington Library.

FOREWORD

The garden, China's foremost environmental art, matured around the mid- to late Ming period, during the sixteenth and seventeenth centuries. Combining the marvels of nature's mountains and rivers with the ingenuity of human skills and artistry, the garden fosters two major modes of enjoyment: solitude and society. It soothes worldly cares and anxieties and stimulates poetic and artistic sensibilities; it is a place to escape into solitude as well as a stage for elegant gatherings of like-minded persons. From the corner of a pavilion one can catch a glimpse of distant mountains; with the sound of rippling water one can dream of a winding stream. Liu Fang Yuan, the Huntington's Chinese Garden, is literally a dream come true. With the combination of a benign climate, a century of horticultural expertise, and ample space at a choice location, a marvelous garden has been waiting to be born. What a wonderful focal point joining the cultures of two great nations across the Pacific!

There is no more pleasurable way to learn about Chinese culture than by strolling in a beautifully designed and expertly constructed classical Chinese garden, splendidly filled with a variety of trees and flowers native to China. This is total immersion, with sights, sounds, and fragrances enticing you to reach deeper into the art, literature, and way of life of this ancient cultural tradition.

As a native of Changshu, which is adjacent to Suzhou, the center of classical Chinese gardens, I have fond memories of visiting these enchanting gardens before I came to the New World in 1938. Thirty years later, I staged the exhibition "Gardens in Chinese Art" at the China Institute in America in New York City. In 2006, June Li, the curator of Liu Fang Yuan, invited me to give the opening lecture on the eve of the completion of the lake phase of the new garden. Many of the paintings that I inherited portray Chinese gardens, and some were included in the Huntington's exhibition that year, "Chrysanthemums on the Eastern Hedge." I also participated in naming the garden Liu Fang Yuan, and was asked to write the calligraphy for its entrance.

In the tenth decade of my life, I am fortunate to associate myself with such a grand undertaking, the creation of a Chinese garden at the Huntington. It is my honor and pleasure to contribute this brief foreword in anticipation of many joyous moments, either in solitude or among gatherings, in the best Chinese garden outside the land of my birth!

Wan–go H. C. Weng
Scholar, collector, and advisory committee member, Liu Fang Yuan

LIU FANG YUAN,
the CHINESE GARDEN *at the* HUNTINGTON

T. June Li

Liu Fang Yuan 流芳園, the Garden of Flowing Fragrance, has transformed about twelve acres of previously undeveloped grounds at the Huntington. At the garden's center is a lake measuring more than an acre, nestled against a densely wooded hollow. An undulating wall on the east side of the garden stakes out its semi-private realm. Lattice windows punctuating the wall at regular intervals offer visitors glimpses into an enchanting world of tiled-roof pavilions and corridors, arched and zigzag bridges, and craggy rocks. Delicately carved bricks decorate the main entrance of the garden. Above the wooden gate, a carved stone plaque proclaims "Liu Fang Yuan." This garden, unique at the Huntington, not only highlights Chinese plants but also serves as a showcase for traditional Chinese architecture and culture.

Thanks to the help of the garden's advisory committee, consisting of Wan-go H. C. Weng, Richard Strassberg, and Yang Ye, all of the major structures have been given Chinese names that provide poetic inspiration or layered references. The name Liu Fang Yuan suggests the presence of flowers and plants that surround and inhabit the garden, or *yuan* 園. *Fang* 芳, meaning fragrance, refers not just to the plant aromas but also specifically to flowers.[1] *Liu* 流,

---

1. See p. 50 of Richard Strassberg's essay.

Attributed to Gu Kaizhi (Chinese, ca. 345–406, Jin dynasty), *The Goddess of the Luo River*, detail, a Song dynasty (960–1279) copy. Handscroll, ink and color on silk; 27.1 x 572.8 cm. The Palace Museum, Beijing, People's Republic of China.

or flowing, actively describes the movement of *fang*, the pleasant scents in the garden. *Liu* also plays on another word, *liu* 留, or lingering, and provides a playful alternative meaning suggesting lasting fragrance in the garden.

The phrase *liu-fang* has a long history in Chinese literature. Cao Zhi 曹植 (192–232) appears to have used it first, in his famous poem *Rhapsody on the Luo River Goddess* (*Luoshen fu* 洛神賦). Describing the goddess, he writes: "She treads in the strong pungency of pepper-plant paths / Walks through clumps of scented flora, allowing their fragrance to flow."[2] The image of a goddess scattering floral scents perfectly characterizes the way that botanical aromas permeate the Chinese Garden. Like the title of a Chinese painting, Liu Fang Yuan beckons the viewer-visitor to enter and enjoy its sensory offerings, prompting identification with the elegant landscapes of the garden's namesake, the great Ming painter Li Liufang 李流芳 (1575–1629).

THE HUNTINGTON BOTANICAL GARDENS

Liu Fang Yuan is the most recent addition to the world-famous Huntington Botanical Gardens. More than a hundred years ago, railroad and real estate developer Henry E. Huntington (1850–1927) began collecting rare and exotic plants for his estate. William Hertrich (1878–1966), his garden superintendent, encouraged Huntington's enthusiasm for interesting

---

2. Cao Zhi, *Luoshen fu, Siku quanshu* ed., 3.3. For an English translation, see Stephen Owen, ed. and trans., *An Anthology of Chinese Literature: Beginnings to 1911*, 1st ed. (New York: W. W. Norton, 1996), 194–97.

每愛練林平遠山
傚迂筝籗落人間幽
人品博雅佳　寫去
春風水一灣　兹岩
喜日忽此図囫題扈
句　李流芳
[seals]

Li Liufang (Chinese, 1575–1629, Ming dynasty), *Thin Forest and Distant Mountains*, 1628. Hanging scroll, ink on paper; 114.3 x 40.3 cm. ©The Cleveland Museum of Art, John L. Severance Fund 1953.630.

Henry E. Huntington's Oriental Garden, ca. 1912.

The Japanese Garden in 2008.

botanical species and built many important botanical collections. The Desert Garden, for example, begun in 1907, is renowned for its dazzling array of cacti and succulents. After Huntington's death, Hertrich and his successors continued to collect a rich variety of plants, resulting in the many specialty gardens found at the Huntington today.[3]

Another gem designed by Hertrich is the Japanese Garden, originally called the Oriental Garden. In it, Hertrich highlighted some Asian plants but also included others, acquired as a whole in 1911 from a Pasadena tea garden owned by George T. Marsh.[4] With the addition of a Japanese house, also purchased from Marsh, an arched wooden bridge, and a *torii* 鳥居 gate, the Oriental Garden became more of a theme garden than a specialized botanical collection. The vogue in Europe and America for the exotic offerings of Japan and other Asian countries influenced the art, music, and literature of the time. At the Huntington, this fashionable trend was embodied in the Oriental Garden. Since the 1950s, it has gradually grown into an elegant Japanese-style garden, with refined aesthetic sensibilities.[5] Today, the Japanese Garden is still an icon of its time, encapsulating the glamour and spirit of the age when the Huntington estate was founded.

The prospect of having a Chinese garden on the grounds of the Huntington began to take shape in the late 1980s, when James Folsom became acting director of the Botanical Gardens.[6] Folsom's interest in following an earlier plan to build a lake in a water runoff depression on the property led him to think about the plantings around such a lake. He decided that a grouping of deciduous trees with stunning autumn colors would create a seasonal landscape that is rarely represented in Southern California. The cooler microclimate of the natural hollow suited a great many of the colorful trees native to China, such as the ginkgo, maple, and pistache. In time, the concept of highlighting Chinese plants, many of them already abundant on the grounds of the Huntington, moved toward a working plan.

The Chinese Garden, created a century after the first gardens at the Huntington were established, reflects today's world, in which cultures maintain their distinctiveness while interacting and mixing. Although the Chinese Garden follows the Huntington tradition of highlighting native plants suitable for each special garden, Liu Fang Yuan does so within its own cultural context, embracing Chinese traditions in authentic ways. With its traditional Chinese buildings and plants, it is unique among the botanical gardens at the Huntington.

THE MAPPING OF LIU FANG YUAN

Just like historical gardens in China, Liu Fang Yuan was conceived with careful attention to the lay of the land. Ji Cheng, a painter and garden designer in seventeenth-century China, wrote an important garden-building manual, the only one from its time known to survive.[7] He noted, "In laying the foundations of a garden you should not feel any restriction as to the direction it faces; the shape of the ground will have its natural highs and lows. There should be

---

3. William Hertrich wrote many books on the botanical collections. For example, see *The Huntington Botanical Gardens, 1905–1949: Personal Recollections of William Hertrich* (San Marino, Calif.: Huntington Library, 1949); and *Camellias in the Huntington Gardens*, 3 vols. (San Marino, Calif.: Huntington Botanical Gardens, 1954–59).

4. For more on the making of the Japanese Garden, see *The Botanical Gardens at the Huntington*, 2nd ed. (San Marino, Calif.: Huntington Library, 2006), 113–23.

5. The Japanese Garden fell into disrepair by World War II. The San Marino League was a major force in bringing the dilapidated garden back to life in the 1950s. Since then, continuous restoration projects imperceptibly transformed the garden and reintroduced the sensitivity of Japanese aesthetics.

6. James Folsom became director of the Botanical Gardens in 1991.

7. Ji Cheng's *Yuan Ye* was written between 1631 and 1634. See Ji Cheng, *The Craft of Gardens*, trans. Alison Hardie (New Haven: Yale University Press, 1988).

something to arouse interest as you pass through the gate; you should follow the natural lay of the land to obtain interesting views."[8]

As mentioned previously, the site for the Chinese Garden is a natural depression for water runoff, surrounded by large, old trees that include native California oaks and many different pine species. When water collects after heavy rains, the site attracts herons, egrets, and families of ducks—as if they were claiming the temporary "lake" as home. On the south side, a lush canyon of camellias, azaleas, and *Prunus* slopes down toward the Japanese Garden. This natural beauty greatly impressed and inspired the designers of the Chinese Garden.[9]

Ji Cheng also noted that "the most important element in the layout of gardens is the siting of the principal buildings. The primary consideration is the view."[10] In Liu Fang Yuan, the placement of the pavilions, bridges, and covered corridors affords the best scenic views of the garden and the distant San Gabriel Mountains. In the lush canyon to the south, a small thatched-roof pavilion poised over the stream flowing toward the Japanese Garden provides dramatic views of the rocky cascade, amid a bucolic retreat. Architectural details include the names of the structures as well as poems, carved on wooden placards and rocks, that were composed and written by calligraphers and friends of the garden.[11] Just like inscriptions on Chinese paintings, these not only highlight scenic views but also provide literary allusions to deeper layers of meaning and cultural nuances.[12]

THE DESIGN OF LIU FANG YUAN

Liu Fang Yuan emulates the refined style of gardens constructed in Suzhou during the Ming (1368–1644) and Qing (1644–1911) periods, which represent some of the high points of garden building in China.[13] In the fifteenth to seventeenth centuries, much wealth, mostly among merchant families, was concentrated in Jiangnan 江南,

Scenic view looking south down the lush canyon at the Pavilion for Washing Away Thoughts.

8. Ibid., 44–45.
9. See p. 29 of Laurie Sowd's essay and p. 82 of James Folsom's essay.
10. Ji, *The Craft of Gardens*, 54.
11. See Appendix C for a list of the names and brief biographies of the calligrapher-poets.
12. See Richard Strassberg's and Yang Ye's essays.
13. See Jerome Silbergeld, "Beyond Suzhou: Region and Memory in the Gardens of Sichuan," *The Art Bulletin* 86, no. 2 (2004): 207–27. Recent scholarship distinguishes many period and regional styles of gardens in China. This topic was discussed at the symposium "Styles of Chinese Gardens," held at the Huntington on June 16, 2007.

Wu Bin (Chinese, active 1573–1620, Ming dynasty), *Mi Wanzhong's Shao Garden*, detail, dated 1615. Handscroll, ink and color on paper; 31 x 356 cm. Wan-go H. C. Weng Collection.

the area south of the Yangzi River.[14] Suzhou was among the most affluent of cities, and its wealthy residents built many beautiful gardens. These residential gardens were private retreats as well as symbols of privilege that revealed their owners' deep resources in a refined manner. Many famous garden estates in Suzhou housed the art and book collections amassed by their owners.[15] In several respects, this affluent class was not too different from its later Western counterpart. In the case of Henry E. Huntington, his wealth from railroads and real estate allowed him to collect impressive works of art, manuscripts, and rare books, and to build extraordinary gardens on his estate.

Large or small, Suzhou gardens feature intimate spatial proportions, which are reflected in the pavilions in Liu Fang Yuan. The delicate wood and stone carved details in the various buildings also reveal the fine craftsmanship of Suzhou, a city long recognized for its famous lapidarian masters as well as carvers of bamboo, wood, ivory, and other materials. All the building components for Liu Fang Yuan, including roof tiles, wood, paving stones, granite bridges, and decorative carvings, were brought from Suzhou. The craggy rocks in the garden are from the area around Tai Hu 太湖, the lake near Suzhou that supplied many famous gardens for over a thousand years.[16] Over sixty master craftsmen in rock and wood, rock designers, and specialists in traditional architecture from Suzhou worked on Liu Fang Yuan, blending thousand-year-old building techniques with modern technology and building codes.[17]

14. See John T. Meskill, *Gentlemanly Interests and Wealth on the Yangtze Delta* (Ann Arbor, Mich.: Association for Asian Studies, 1994).
15. Manuals of taste were influential in the fifteenth to seventeenth centuries among the wealthy gentry seeking to appear cultivated. For a translation of one of these "manuals" and a discussion of the social antics of this period, see Craig Clunas, *Superfluous Things: Material Culture and Social Status in Early Modern China* (Urbana, Ill.: University of Illinois Press, 1991).
16. For more about Tai Hu rock and other prized rocks, see Robert D. Mowry et al., *Worlds within Worlds: The Richard Rosenblum Collection of Chinese Scholars' Rocks* (Cambridge, Mass.: Harvard University Art Museums, 1997).
17. See Laurie Sowd's essay on p. 32.

Lake of Reflected Fragrance.

Liu Fang Yuan is not modeled on any specific Suzhou garden. Rather, it follows the centuries-old guidelines of garden designers such as Ji Cheng, preserving what is already on the chosen site while creating new landscape compositions and views. Accordingly, Liu Fang Yuan is distinctive for its groves of old oak trees, natives of Southern California that have inhabited the grounds for close to a century.[18]

Like the many Ming and Qing gardens designed as paintings, Liu Fang Yuan contains the major elements of a Chinese landscape painting, or *shan shui hua* 山水畫. As microcosms of the universe, landscape paintings always include mountain/rocks (*shan*) and water (*shui*), with architectural structures often indicating human participation. Liu Fang Yuan represents this paradigm of the universe with its Tai Hu rocks, distant San Gabriel Mountains, Lake of Reflected Fragrance, Chinese plants, and old native trees. Pavilions invite visitors to participate in this three-dimensional painting and enjoy its scenic compositions, poetic inscriptions, and calligraphy.

The following essays are records, or *yuanji* 園記, of Liu Fang Yuan. The authors have each participated and contributed to the making of the garden. *Liu Fang Yuan Yuanji* documents the creation, building, design, naming, and planting of the Chinese Garden at the Huntington.

T. June Li is the Curator of Liu Fang Yuan.

---

18. See James Folsom's essay on p. 81 for more about the plants in Liu Fang Yuan.

Framed view through the Terrace of the Jade Mirror.

Framed view from the Love for the Lotus Pavilion.

水流云在

Preliminary drawing for the Chinese Garden, by Jin Chen.

THE MAKING *of* LIU FANG YUAN:

A BRIEF HISTORY

Laurie Sowd

Liu Fang Yuan, its first phase now open to visitors, has been more than twenty years in the making—close to the amount of time it took to create some of the famous Suzhou gardens of the Ming and Qing periods. A Chinese garden at the Huntington, first thought of in the late 1980s as a showcase for Chinese plants, began to take shape in the mid-1990s, when Frances Tsu, a professor of Chinese architecture, and Bob Ray Offenhauser, a Los Angeles architect, drew initial conceptual plans.

In 2001, Jin Chen, a Chinese-American landscape architect, joined the staff of the Huntington, and over the following two years developed a master plan for the garden and articulated many of the features that are evident today. At the same time, the Huntington hired Chinese design and construction companies to work with the American architect and the general contractor. In the fall of 2004, construction began on the utilities and lake, and 2006 and 2007 saw construction of the pavilions, bridges, and covered walkways of the first phase. Finally, in February 2008 Liu Fang Yuan opened to the public.

EAST-WEST COLLABORATION

Capturing the authentic spirit of a Suzhou-style private garden meant working with Chinese experts in the fields of design, materials, construction, and craftsmanship. In the fall of 2001, Huntington staff interviewed five companies in Suzhou, Shanghai, and Beijing that

American and Chinese architects worked together to resolve design challenges.

Chinese artisans at work in China, preparing elements for shipment to the Huntington. Hand tools are used in wood-carving (above); artisans add texture to solid granite elements (top).

had expertise in classical Chinese garden design in order to find one to translate Chen's overall conceptual plan into working drawings. We also talked to five Chinese construction companies about applying their knowledge from centuries of craftsmanship to the building of the garden. After seeing samples of their elegant and thoughtful work, we selected the Suzhou Institute of Landscape Architecture Design, led by He Fengchun, and the Suzhou Garden Development Company, guided by senior engineer Lu Hongren.

The Suzhou design firm brought its skills to bear on the selection of decorative motifs, the framing of scenery, and the layering of views. Because the Suzhou architects were not licensed to practice in the United States, however, their drawings could not be submitted for the required construction permits. An American architectural firm, Offenhauser and Associates, led by Jim Fry (pictured above, left), turned the Suzhou design into engineered construction documents, presented in both metric and imperial measurement systems, with notes in Chinese and English.

The Suzhou construction firm helped shape the design process as well, offering insights into how the structures might be built. The company's other roles included purchasing materials in China (with the exception of structural steel, concrete, some paving pebbles, and miscellaneous plywood, all of the building materials came from China); and fabricating bridges, pavilions, decorative panels, paving bricks, and roof tiles in their Suzhou workshops. Finally, they packed and shipped the prefabricated materials to the Huntington and sent artisans here to assemble and install them.

Just as we needed an architect licensed in California to submit plans for permitting, we required an American contractor to build the infrastructure of the garden and support the work

Suzhou artisans build a curved roof.

of the artisans. For this we engaged ValleyCrest Landscape Development Company, a nationally recognized landscape firm with extensive experience in civil and other construction projects. ValleyCrest's first responsibility was to build the infrastructure of the site. They installed pipes and utilities under and around the lake for its elaborate biofiltration and pumping system, and electrical conduits to power lighting and irrigation.

The lakebed is composed of heavily compacted earth and a plastic liner topped with concrete that is stained to mimic a natural soil bank. The integrity of the waterproof membrane liner was a major consideration, so the footings and foundations of all lake-adjacent structures were built at the same time, allowing the liner to

Hand-carved solid granite bridges are installed on their foundations.

Structural steel forms the skeleton of the tea house, the future Hall of the Jade Camellia.

wrap around the footings and ensure water tightness. Consequently, this first phase of building included foundations for structures that are planned for future phases of the garden.

Suzhou artisans installed the bridges on the concrete footings. ValleyCrest continued to pour foundations for all pavilions, covered walkways, and terraces, and they erected the structural steel skeleton of the buildings. A few months later, Suzhou artisans returned to assemble the wood pavilions, tile roofs, and decorative paving.

DESIGN CHALLENGES

The goal of authenticity brought practical challenges that required innovative solutions. These challenges included designing and engineering traditional-style pavilions and bridges that would withstand Southern California earthquakes, meeting other building code requirements, and selecting appropriate materials.

Before we could begin the actual work of designing the garden, we had to reach an agreement with our new colleagues. Though the Suzhou design company had signed memos of understanding on other projects, they were unfamiliar with components of our legal contract, which dealt in detail with issues such as ownership of documents, tax withholding, penalties for failure to perform, intellectual property rights, insurance coverage, and applicable law and language. Even with the help of a Mandarin-speaking Chinese-American attorney, it took nearly a year to negotiate the first contract with the Suzhou design company as we developed mutual trust and an understanding of each others' priorities. The Chinese and American design teams then set to work collaborating on how to meet a number of building code requirements, including those for structural engineering, guardrails, accessibility, fire suppression, and health department policies.

A mock-up of the roof shows layers of wood, waterproofing, and tiles.

Densely overlaid baked clay tiles are installed on a pavilion roof.

Chinese pavilions are typically constructed of wood columns and beams that support multi-layered tile roofs about four times heavier than typical American residential roofs. All the columns and structural beams in the garden's pavilions had to be made of steel to meet the structural requirements for Southern California, one of the most active seismic zones in the United States. At the same time, we were committed to preserving the proportions and traditional appearance of the buildings with the texture and feel of wood materials. One of the most significant challenges to our design and construction collaboration was figuring out how to encase structural steel with decoratively carved wood in a way that would allow the beautiful traditional joinery to be the predominant feature. We labored over this issue for nearly two years, using a series of models to guide us toward a number of customized solutions. Column-length wood wraps encase the steel columns of the finished pavilions; almost every beam detail required an individual solution for attaching the decorative wood around the steel.

Building codes also dictate that bridges arching high above water must have guardrail-height banisters—much higher than those used in traditional Chinese architecture. In addition, openings in those railings cannot exceed four inches. This requirement affected the proportions

Prefabricated wood "wraps" for encasing structural steel columns.

Stone bases are added to the column below the wood wrap.

Wood beams, shown above and below, are fitted around structural steel.

The removable threshold of the tea house allows access while preserving traditional design.

Building code requires banisters on the Jade Ribbon Bridge to be guardrail-height.

aesthetically, causing some bridges to appear heavier and taller than they do in traditional architecture.

Another design challenge came as we addressed code requirements and our own institutional commitment to accessibility. For example, should we include thresholds—a key design feature in Chinese garden pavilions—even though they inhibit access by requiring the visitor to step over a six-inch wood element? Collaboration resulted in a creative, practical approach—thresholds on key access routes are removable, so that visitors can see the original design when appropriate, and have unhindered access otherwise.

Our tea shop, "The Freshwater Pavilion," contains a food preparation area that had to meet requirements for fire-suppression systems and nonporous ceilings, floors, walls, and countertops. Collegial discussions with governing agencies and innovative design led to the use of fire sprinklers with side-throw heads—so as not to block the view of the decorative ceiling beams—and the incorporation of a nonporous soffit just over the cooking area, again allowing maximum visibility and appreciation of the traditional architecture.

BUILDING ELEMENTS AND MATERIALS

The garden's distinctive dark-gray roof tiles (and all other baked-clay elements, including floor bricks) are made from a yellow clay that is abundant in the regions south of the Yangzi, including the area around Suzhou. This clay is mixed with water and put into molds such as those that were used for making the chrysanthemum-motif roof tiles (see page 64 for the pattern). The clay is then baked in a brick kiln fired with rice straw. As

Artisans place individual pebbles to create decorative paving, using a refined traditional motif.

the temperature rises gradually and the bricks bake for about forty days, the tiles take on an intense gray color from the smoke and ash.

Another notable feature is the lattice windows, or *lou chuang* 漏窗. The artisans began the fabrication of each window by drawing a lacy design on a flat board and outlining it with nails. Then they wrapped a fine wire mesh around the nails, using that as a base for applying layers of plaster to build up the window. The windows are then installed in the walls, through which they offer a glimpse of the garden beyond.

Decorative paving is a traditional characteristic of Chinese gardens. The artisans outlined traditional designs using the edges of roof tiles, and then individually placed round, flat pebbles on their ends to fill in the patterns. After completing the pattern on dry mortar, they poured water on it to set the paving designs and create a safe, stable surface.

Nails and wire mesh outline the pattern of the lattice windows.

The wire pattern is coated with multiple layers of plaster.

The lattice windows, ready to be installed.

The lattice windows installed in the garden wall.

The selection of materials also brought a number of challenges. The bridges in the garden are made of hand-carved, solid granite from China. Before making a final selection of stone, we had to verify the material's strength for the local building department by shipping some pieces to the United States and engaging a laboratory to test them.

Wood pavilions carved of fir, ginkgo, fragrant camphor, and cypress pose practical considerations for maintenance and durability. We wondered why wood finishes in other Chinese gardens in North America showed significant cracking and peeling. One reason could be a fundamental incompatibility between the lead-based primers applied in China before shipping (crucial to protecting the wood during trans-ocean travel) and the paints used in the United States. To prevent this problem, we sent American primers to Suzhou for application before the wood elements were shipped and domestic paint was applied when the materials arrived. Time will tell whether our strategy was successful.

Another maintenance issue was the difficulty of cleaning the lattice carved-wood details on windows and doors. Our innovative solution involved hinging the wood lattice to swing away from the glass for cleaning. We hope this kind of pioneering collaboration will be of some benefit to our Suzhou colleagues as well.

HOSTING THE ARTISANS

Over the course of the construction, we hosted sixty artisans from Suzhou for periods of two to six months. They ranged in age from twenty-six to sixty, and all had advanced certifications as skilled artisans, high-level carpenters, or expert stonemasons.

The Chinese companies did not have contractor licenses that allowed them to do construction work in the United States, so ValleyCrest hired the artisans as their own employees—reflecting a true commitment to this international collaboration. By doing so, ValleyCrest took responsibility for the artisans' safety, workers compensation insurance, and payroll; the company also provided them with tools, uniforms, and boots. The work teams spoke Mandarin, English, and Spanish on the site. A shared understanding of the work to be accomplished ensured that sign language largely sufficed, and Valley Crest employed several translators who were available during construction hours.

There were practical challenges in hosting the artisans: finding appropriate accommodations (through a wonderful hotel where Mandarin is spoken in one of the many Chinese communities around the Huntington); providing meals (Chinese box lunches catered to the Huntington each day); and allowing for recreational activities (a "community room" with ping-pong table and refrigerator helped ease the transition into group residential life; donors and community members hosted barbeques, architectural tours, and concert evenings. Venice Beach, Hollywood, Universal Studios and Las

Hinged windows were constructed to allow easy cleaning around decorative wood lattice.

English, Spanish, and Mandarin speakers work together to place rocks from Lake Tai.

Vegas were favorite destinations.) Birthday parties, complete with cake, candles, and "Happy Birthday" sung in two languages, provided needed celebrations.

The contributions of the Chinese artisans were essential, both to the authenticity of Liu Fang Yuan and to its success in the Southern California setting of the Huntington. One key feature of the garden is its collection of Lake Tai rocks—850 tons of craggy, sculptural limestone rocks that highlight the lake edge and form a waterfall. They are unique to the Suzhou area and therefore essential for inclusion in this garden. The artisans placed the rocks as if they had sprung from the earth—an aesthetic that could not have been duplicated by local craftsmen. This happened early in the construction process, and convinced us that hosting artisans from China was a critical element for the project. The design and construction of Liu Fang Yuan called upon and truly brought out the best in all team members—creativity, good will, patience, and a vision for and commitment to creating a unique place of cultural memory at the Huntington.

Just as garden owners in the Ming dynasty did, we are living with the structures in our garden, seeing how they work with the landscape to frame the views, and observing how our visitors experience this marvelous place. Armed with this insight, we are shaping the next phase of construction, considering what other structures and plants are needed to allow the garden to serve a variety of functions and to complete this three-dimensional landscape painting.

Laurie Sowd is the Huntington's Associate Vice President for Operations and the project director for Liu Fang Yuan.

Lake Tai rocks add dramatic views to the garden.

THE NECESSITY *of* NAMES *in* CHINESE GARDENS

◇ Richard E. Strassberg

The attachment of names to gardens is a worldwide phenomenon that can be traced back to the myths, epics, sacred texts, and inscriptions of antiquity. Many of these names have denoted geographical locations, identified individual owners, or served purely descriptive purposes. Others have become generalized in meaning—Eden, for example, signifying paradise. Yet, many gardens outside of China and East Asia do not depend on specific names or literary associations to be understood and enjoyed. Their cultural meanings are primarily communicated through elements such as architecture, sculpture, landscape design, and plants. Western gardens in a succession of exotic and historical styles—Baroque, neoclassical, English, Moorish, and even Chinese—have transmitted distinct associations that were immediately recognizable, without the context that a name might confer. Moreover, since the eighteenth-century development of the "natural" garden in England, the inclusion of words and themes in a scene has sometimes been regarded as an artificial intrusion by civilization that interferes with a desire to experience wilderness.

By contrast, an authentically Chinese garden is designed to be read through the medium of language in order to convey its unique identity. The presence of signs written in fine calligraphy reveals the deeper meaning of a scene (*jing* 景), for myths credit the origin of writing to the observation of natural forms by ancient sages. The necessity of defining a particular

"Natural" garden design in Stowe, England. South front of Stowe landscape gardens.
© The National Trust Photo Library, UK/Rupert Truman.

Chinese garden's character through names may be due to the generic quality of its basic design elements. These include standardized forms of traditional architecture, a specific repertoire of symbolic plants, and omnipresent objects such as monumental rocks. Creating a garden without inscribing it would be like painting a landscape without assigning it a title or accompanying poem; it would be like drawing a dragon without "dotting its pupils," as the Chinese saying goes, to bring it to life. In China's greatest classic novel *The Story of the Stone* (*Shitouji* 石頭記, ca. 1750), the character Jia Zheng 賈政 famously remarks upon inspecting the family's newly constructed garden, "All those prospects and pavilions—even the rocks and trees and flowers will seem somehow incomplete without that touch of poetry which only the written word can lend a scene."[1] Conferring names is an obligation of the educated elite that is connected on the broadest level with the maintenance of order in society, the state, and the cosmos. One of the expressions for "building a garden," *zhiyuan* 治園, literally means "governing a garden," which is achieved by correlating its patterns with the macro-structures of Chinese civilization. Confucius (551–479 BCE) himself charged the scholar-official class with "rectifying names" (*zhengming* 正名)—that is, correctly applying language to aspects of reality in order to stabilize the world. While Daoist and Buddhist thinkers remained skeptical of language's ability to signify truth objectively and permanently, they nevertheless invented a wide range of names as useful tools in the pursuit of spiritual transcendence. Chinese gardens

---

1. Cao Xueqin, *The Story of the Stone*, trans. David Hawkes, vol. 1 (Harmondsworth, U.K.: Penguin Books, 1973), 324–25. The novel is also known as *Hongloumeng* 紅樓夢, *The Dream of the Red Chamber*, or *A Dream of Red Mansions*.

Zhao Boju (Chinese, ca. 1120–1162, Song dynasty), *The Han Palace*, undated. Album leaf, ink and color on silk; 24.5 x 24.5 cm. National Palace Museum, Taipei, Taiwan, Republic of China.

Qiu Ying (Chinese, 1494–1552, Ming dynasty), *The Garden for Self-Enjoyment* (or the *Garden of Solitary Delight*), detail, 1515–52. Handscroll, ink and slight color on silk; 27.8 x 381 cm. © The Cleveland Museum of Art, John L. Severance Fund 1978.67.

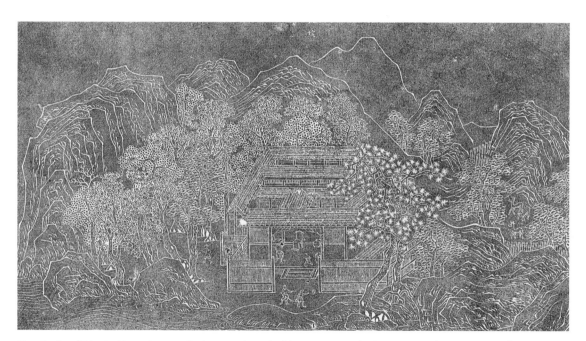

Shen Guohua (Chinese, fifteenth century), after Guo Zhongshu (Chinese, 910–977), after Wang Wei (Chinese 701–761), *Wangchuan Villa*, detail, Tang dynasty, 618–907. Handscroll, ink rubbing on paper; 30 x 496.7 cm. Princeton University Art Museum.

invoke the rich lexicons of the "three teachings," and function like highly allusive texts that refer to famous landscapes, other notable gardens, great personalities, lyric poetry, fiction, drama, and myth, as well as the visual and performing arts.

In earlier periods, imperial gardens with their palatial buildings displayed the most imaginative and impressive names, such as the Palace of Everlasting Joy 長樂 and the Garden of Glorious Breezes 光風園 of the Han dynasty (206 BCE–220 CE). These gardens were designed to create a microcosm of the universe centered on the ruler, and they were celebrated in rhetorically intricate court poetry. Private gardens, particularly large, rural estates, often employed more modest names based on perceptions of the local scenery. Influential poems by individual landowners, such as the rhapsody by Xie Lingyun 謝靈運 (385–443) about his large estate at Shining ("Shanju fu" 山居賦) and the cycle of poems by Wang Wei 王維 (701–761) concerning his rural villa at Wangchuan ("Wangchuan ji bing xu" 輞川集並序), provide details of specific scenes and evoke their lyrical ambience while mapping itineraries.[2] In both cases, formal names would have been indicated by placards placed above gates or doorways, or by engravings on rocks.

An important literary genre that arose among men of letters in the Tang dynasty (618–907) was the garden record, or *yuanji* 園記. A prose essay in classical Chinese, it presented a variety of information that might include the history and design of the garden, the character

2. For a study and translation of Xie Lingyun's poem, see Francis Abeken Westbrook, "Landscape Description in the Lyric Poetry and 'Fuh on Dwelling in the Mountains' of Shieh Ling-Yunn" (PhD diss., Yale University, 1972). For a translation of Wang Wei's cycle, see *Laughing Lost in the Mountains: Poems of Wang Wei*, trans. Tony Barnstone, Willis Barnstone, and Xu Haixin (Hanover, N.H.: University Press of New England, 1991), 25–34.

After Xie Huan (Chinese, ca. 1370–ca. 1450, Ming dynasty), *Elegant Gathering in the Apricot Garden*, detail, ca. 1437. Handscroll, ink and color on silk; 37.5 x 240.7 cm. The Metropolitan Museum of Art, Purchase, The Dillon Fund Gift, 1989 (1989.141.3).

Jia Baoyu and Jia Zheng discussing the name for what will be called the Pavilion of Drenched Blossoms. In Sun Wen's (Chinese, act. nineteenth century, Qing dynasty) album, *A Dream of Red Mansions,* also known as *The Story of the Stone,* ca. 1867–1903. Album leaf, ink and color on silk; 41 x 75.2 cm. Lüshun Museum, Dalian, People's Republic of China.

and ideals of the owner, the significance of the garden's names, and a tour of its notable scenes. Being in a garden was conceived of as a programmed journey through an ideal landscape, and the garden record owes many of its literary conventions to the travel record (*youji* 遊記), a parallel genre that appeared around the same time. Garden records were composed by the owners themselves, or by famous writers, and some have become widely read works of literature. They might commemorate an occasion, such as the writer's own visit, or serve as a formal description that preserves a fixed image of the garden for posterity long after the garden has been altered or has disappeared. Indeed, the famous gardens of the past are now mostly known to us through these records, along with the paintings and poems that sometimes accompanied these writings. In many of the gardens that survive, it is not uncommon today to see such a record on a wall at the entrance or printed in a guidebook.[3]

One of the most famous examples, "A Record of the Garden of Solitary Delight" (*Duleyuan ji* 獨樂園記) by the influential Northern Song dynasty scholar-official Sima Guang 司馬光 (1019–1086), focuses on defending his un-Confucian choice for a garden name. Creating a reclusive persona, he playfully attempts to counter charges of selfishness and asserts his right to a private space away from the concerns of public life. The scenes he names and describes, including a library of some five thousand books, are all places for enjoying a refuge from the cares of the world. Actually, Sima Guang was centrally engaged in the court politics of his time, and he owned other, larger gardens that served as his principal residences. The Garden of Solitary Delight was a small retreat he built in Luoyang in 1073 when he was out of power but still enjoyed imperial favor. The fame of this garden and the success of his record among readers helped further sanction the use of gardens by the ascendant scholar-official class as autonomous spaces for the pursuit of self-cultivation.[4]

An important change in the practice of naming gardens took place with the spread of private gardens, particularly in the Jiangnan region, from the Ming dynasty (1368–1644) on. While the most notable earlier gardens were largely open to the landscape around them, later gardens, especially smaller sites in crowded urban areas such as Suzhou, generally turned inward and made use of illusionistic effects to enhance the perception of space and capture a sense of natural grandeur.[5] As writing, publishing, and literacy greatly increased, gardens were employed to signify the cultural prestige and social status of their owners. An ideal lifestyle of leisure (*xianqing* 閑情) was pursued in gardens, which were represented as spaces for sociability, pleasure, and artistic creativity.

Names proliferated and became more learned in their references, and the practice of adding poetic couplets (*duilian* 對聯) gained popularity. A couplet is composed of two lines of poetry, usually five or seven characters long, that match each other in diction, syntax, and imagery to frame a balanced, lyrical world. These lines are written vertically (with the columns to be read from right to left), usually in calligraphy, by a notable artist or personality. Then

---

3. For recently published anthologies of garden records in Chinese and French respectively, see Chen Zhi 陈植 and Zhang Gongchi 张公驰, eds., *Zhongguo lidai mingyuanji xuanzhu* 中国历代名园记选注 [Selected, Annotated Records of Famous Gardens through History] (Hefei, China: Anhui kexue jishu chubanshe, 1983); and Martine Vallette-Hémery, *Les Paradis Naturels: Jardins Chinois en Prose* (Arles: Phillipe Picquier, 2001).

4. See Sima Guang, "The Garden of Solitary Delight," in Ji Cheng, *The Craft of Gardens*, trans. Alison Hardie (New Haven: Yale University Press, 1988), 123–24.

5. For a discussion of this shift and its implications for interior design, see Wang Yi, "Interior Display and Its Relation to External Spaces in Traditional Chinese Gardens," *Studies in the History of Gardens & Designed Landscapes* 18, no. 3 (1998): 232–47.

they are inscribed on wooden plaques affixed to the pillars forming the entrance to a structure or along both sides of a window. Other formats include stone engravings or ceramic plaques fastened to a wall. The visitor who arrives at a pavilion marking a focal scene, for example, would first read the name of the building on the horizontal placard above, and then the lines of the couplet on each side, in order to understand the deeper significance of the view. After some moments spent in observation and contemplation, visitors might compare their reactions, and even compose further poetry to express their own experience. In this way, the practice of naming was not only an autobiographical expression of the owner's identity or the artistic expression of a talented poet or calligrapher, but also a means for others to become part of an ideal place that was preserved in writing for posterity.

The most complete description of the process of naming and reading a garden can be found in the episode in *The Story of the Stone* mentioned above.[6] When Jia Zheng and his son Baoyu 寶玉 tour the new garden, they append provisional names to its many sights, for the garden has been constructed to serve as a temporary palace for Yuanchun 元春, the eldest daughter, who has become an imperial concubine and has been permitted to return home for a brief family visit. The entire garden has been designed to be read by her, and the various discussions about appropriateness, the use of literary allusion, and the meaning of the natural versus the artificial take place from the point of view of her perceptions. Their intention is not only to delight Yuanchun but also to celebrate the imperial ethos and to subtly remind her of the importance of her role in maintaining the family's aristocratic status. The story shows how naming can also become an act of possession. When Yuanchun arrives and is allowed to tour the garden for a few hours, she exercises her prerogative and makes changes in some of the names according to her taste. There is a telling moment when she reaches the formal stone arch before the main hall. Its provisional name is "Precinct of the Celestial Visitant" (Tianxian baojing 天仙寶境), a clear reference to Yuanchun's semidivine identity. Immediately, she orders it changed to "The House of Reunion" (Xingqin bieshu 省親別墅), revealing her desire to take control of the constraining ritual and escape the golden cage of palace life to re-experience, however briefly, her carefree existence as a daughter in the household. She also bestows the name "Prospect Garden" (Daguanyuan 大觀園) on the garden. Later, Yuanchun announces her intention to write a garden record to be inscribed in stone at the site, in an attempt to preserve the garden as it was during her visit.[7]

The Garden of Flowing Fragrance, Liu Fang Yuan 流芳園, continues the long tradition of Chinese gardens, past and present. It is a unique creation in the Jiangnan style whose name appropriately signifies the Huntington Botanical Gardens' preeminent role among the world's gardens. The word *fang* 芳 (fragrance) is widely used in Chinese lyric poetry and other literary genres to refer to flowers, fragrant plants, and botanicals in general, and it is also used as a metaphor of feminine beauty. The word can be found in the titles of scholarly works such as

---

6. See Cao Xueqin, *The Story of the Stone*, chapters 17–18, pp. 324–74. In the original manuscript of the novel, these formed a single chapter.

7. Though widely known as "Grand View Garden," it is called "Prospect Garden" in Hawkes' translation, cited above. For studies of this fictional garden, which epitomizes the entire tradition of Chinese garden culture, see Andrew H. Plaks, *Archetype and Allegory in "The Dream of the Red Chamber"* ([Princeton]: Princeton University Press, 1976); Xiao Chi, *The Chinese Garden as Lyric Enclave: A Generic Study of "The Story of the Stone"* (Ann Arbor: Center for Chinese Studies Publications, University of Michigan, 2001).

Pavilion for Washing Away Thoughts.

the influential early-thirteenth-century encyclopedia *Quanfang beizu* 全芳備祖 (*Complete Literary References to Plants*). The image of "flowing" (*liu* 流) fragrance invokes one of the most widely used tropes in lyric poetry, that of blossoms flowing along a stream. Chinese gardens embody the paradox of a continual experience of nature together with a poignant sense of the passing of time. In the immortal words of Su Shi 蘇軾 (1037–1101), uttered as he contemplated the inexhaustible Yangzi River, "It flows by yet never leaves us."[8] The Garden of Flowing Fragrance underscores this perception in a double sense: its plants reflect an endless cycle of change through the four seasons, while its ingenious hydraulic engineering actually recirculates the water that appears to cascade away.

Richard E. Strassberg is Professor in the Department of Asian Languages and Cultures at UCLA.

8. Su Shih (Su Shi), "Red Cliff I," in *Inscribed Landscapes: Travel Writing from Imperial China*, trans. Richard E. Strassberg (Berkeley: University of California Press, 1994), 187.

THE IMPLIED VISITOR:

NAMES *and* THEIR MEANINGS *in* LIU FANG YUAN

◇ Yang Ye

Landscape (rocks and water), buildings, and flora constitute the essence of a traditional Chinese garden. The naming of the various architectural structures and scenic spots serves to "set the scene" (*dianjing* 點景), and it has become an increasingly important milestone in the completion of a garden. Finding appropriate names helps breathe life into each particular site and enhance its aesthetic dimensions.

A vivid account of such a naming process is provided in *The Story of the Stone*, in which Jia Zheng 賈政, the paterfamilias of the Rongguo House 榮國府, leads his son Baoyu 寶玉 and a group of retainer-scholars on a walk around the garden that has recently been constructed to celebrate a homecoming visit from his daughter, an imperial concubine. Once the names are finalized, the buildings—especially the residences of the novel's major characters, such as Lin Daiyu's 林黛玉 Naiad's House (Xiaoxiang Guan 瀟湘館), and Xue Baochai's 薛寶釵 All-spice Court (Hengwu Yuan 蘅蕪院)—become an integral part of the novel, and are endowed with almost as much life as the characters living there.[1]

A great challenge of naming sites in the Huntington's Chinese Garden was that, unlike those who assigned the garden names that were recorded in history or literature, the Huntington's advisory committee did not enjoy the luxury of direct, visual inspiration from a completed garden. Instead, the names had to be suggested and adopted far ahead of time. Many a site or structure existed as no more than a mere dot on a blueprint, with the natural scenery at the site serving as a guide for our imagination.

---

1. Cao Xueqin, *The Story of the Stone*, trans. David Hawkes, vol. 1 (Harmondsworth, U.K.: Penguin Books, 1973), chapters 17–18, pp. 324–74.

Sun Wen (Chinese, act. nineteenth century, Qing dynasty), Garden scene from the album *A Dream of Red Mansions,* also known as *The Story of the Stone,* ca. 1867–1903. Album leaf, ink and color on silk; 41 x 75.2 cm. Lüshun Museum, Dalian, People's Republic of China.

Entrance to Plantain Court.

Throughout the process, it seems to me, the advisory committee had a potential visitor in mind. We proposed, suggested, weighed pros and cons, and argued for or against each and every name in the prospective Chinese Garden— including the name eventually chosen for the entire garden, Liu Fang Yuan. The committee took care in selecting these names, imagining an ideal visitor who was not an uninterested viewer. He or she would take an active part in the full composition of the meaning of the names, asking, "What meanings does each name contain?"

Behind every name, I suggest, there exists a blank, a gap, a "spot of indeterminacy"[2] for the visitor to cope with intellectually. To do that, one has to evoke and explore a hidden cultural text of art, history, language, and poetry, which provides the foundation for his or her interpretation. One's particular reaction to a name, as well as the kind of tension arising between the visitor and the puzzle of the name, depends on individual experience, which accounts for the formation of unique horizons of expectation. On the other hand, the cultural text also implies active participation on the part of the visitor, who is by no means apathetic, passive, or static, but rather embarks on a continuous process of discovery. Such an "Implied Visitor," while strolling in the garden, keeps playing a mental game about the names of the various places by questioning and revising expectations established by the cultural text, filling in the blanks, sealing the gaps, and making sense of the spots of indeterminacy contained in the names.[3]

For the Implied Visitor, most of the names in Liu Fang Yuan follow a dictum, a rule that, in the Chinese tradition, finds its expression in Baoyu's argument in the above-mentioned episode of *The Story of the Stone*: "To recall old things is better than to invent new ones; and to recut an ancient text is better than to engrave a modern [one]."[4]

Some of the names in Liu Fang Yuan directly indicate or highlight the locations, surroundings, or themes of the buildings; others use artistic or literary associations that may indirectly expand the aesthetic sphere of the structures—many do both.

---

2. The term "spot of indeterminacy," widely used in literary criticism, was coined by Polish philosopher Roman Witold Ingarden (1893–1970), whose works have been influential in the fields of phenomenology, ontology, and aesthetics.
3. For the idea of the "Implied Visitor" I am indebted to the concept of the "Implied Reader" presented by Wolfgang Iser (1926–2007) in his study of English novels, *Der implizite Leser: Kommunikationsformen des Romans von Bunyan bis Beckett* (Munich: W. Fink, 1972). (There is an English translation by the author, *The Implied Reader: Patterns of Communication in Prose Fiction from Bunyan to Beckett* [Baltimore: Johns Hopkins University Press, 1974].)
4. Cao Xueqin, *The Story of the Stone*, chapter 17, p. 328.

Let us, for the moment, give free rein to our imagination. On a fine, sunny day in late spring, while a soft breeze wafts the fragrance of myriad flowers, which hovers and lingers everywhere, a visitor arrives for an excursion at Liu Fang Yuan. Lynette, who teaches Chinese literature at an East Coast college, is in Los Angeles for a conference and decides to pay a long overdue visit to the garden. She calls her old friend Giles, who lives in nearby Pasadena. Much to her delight, Giles, who shares her love for Chinese culture, happens to be a docent at the Huntington.

Giles is more than happy to give Lynette a tour of Liu Fang Yuan, and they meet at the southern entrance, under the carved stone plaque that bears the garden's name. Once they enter, they see a horizontal tablet above, engraved with four large Chinese characters, Bie You Dong Tian 別有洞天 (Another World Lies Beyond), or more literally, "Another Heaven Inside the Cave." "Heaven Inside the Cave—the Land of the Immortals," Giles says to Lynette, explaining the Daoist term *dong tian* on the tablet.[5] Lynette is quick to associate the name with the beloved literary text "Peach Blossom Spring" 桃花源記 by the ancient poet Tao Yuanming 陶淵明 (365–427). Born into a declining aristocratic family, Tao served briefly as a county magistrate but decided to resign and live a humble but carefree life in the fields and gardens of his homeland. Written by Tao as a companion prose piece to a pentasyllabic poem bearing the same title, "Peach Blossom Spring" tells how a fisherman inadvertently finds a hidden world inside a little hillside cave. People live there in harmony and peace, protected from the world outside and all the social upheavals throughout history. In Chinese tradition, the very term "Peach Blossom Spring" has become synonymous with utopia—the ideal state.[6] Lynette and Giles agree that the inscription "Another World Lies Beyond" serves as an apt introduction to the garden, as it not only reminds them of the beautiful story but

Another World Lies Beyond, just inside the entrance to the garden.

5. An ancient Daoist belief, mentioned in such Daoist books as the *Yunji qiqian* 雲笈七籤 [Classics of Clouds in Seven Sets of Bamboo Slips], was that Immortals were assigned to live in Ten Great Heavens Inside Caves 十大洞天 and Thirty-Six Heavens Inside Caves 三十六洞天. For the Chinese text see Zhang Junfang 張君房, *Yunji qiqian, Siku quanshu* 四庫全書 ed., 27.2, 4.
6. For Cyril Birch's English translation of the prose part of the work, see Cyril Birch, ed., *Anthology of Chinese Literature: From Early Times to the Fourteenth Century* (New York: Grove Press, 1965), 167–68. See also Appendix A, no. 2.

Fan Qi (Chinese, 1616–after 1694) *Peach Blossom Spring*, 1646. From *Landscapes* album of eight leaves. Album leaf, ink and color on paper; 16.8 x 20.3 cm. The Metropolitan Museum of Art, The Sackler Fund, 1969 (69.242.10).

also signifies that by walking through the gate, they are entering a world with a culture and history all its own.

Strolling along the Lake of Reflected Fragrance, they come upon a beautiful lakeside pavilion named Ai Lian Xie 愛蓮榭 (Love for the Lotus Pavilion). This reminds Lynette of "A Note on the Love of Lotus" 愛蓮說, a mini-essay (*xiaopin* 小品) by the Song dynasty philosopher Zhou Dunyi 周敦頤 (1017–1073), who eulogizes the lotus as a symbol of noble purity because, growing up in mud notwithstanding, it preserves its shining whiteness. Giles adds that the lotus is also a Buddhist symbol, described in one of the sutras as a flower with four cardinal virtues: fragrance, purity, softness, and loveliness.[7] According to legend, the seat of the Buddha himself was in the shape of a lotus flower.

A little farther on, they arrive at the double-roofed, hexagonal pavilion east of the lake, San You Ge 三友閣 (Pavilion of the Three Friends). The "three friends of the cold season"—pine, bamboo, and plum (*Prunus mume*)—inspire Lynette and Giles to exchange numerous sayings and stories about their respective symbolism in Chinese art and literature.

Beyond San You Ge, a winding stream flowing into the lake catches their attention. From the rock engraving, Lynette identifies the name Huan Hua Xi 浣花溪 (Flower Washing Brook) as one that harks back to China's greatest poet, Du Fu 杜甫 (712–770). Lynette, who specializes in classical poetry, recalls that Du Fu once lived in a thatched cottage by the side of a similarly meandering stream in Sichuan. Pointing to the colorful petals floating down the brook, Lynette remarks that it was exactly such a beautiful sight in late spring that inspired the poet to name his cottage the "Flower-Washing Cottage." Giles hurries to add that the anonymous stream winding by the cottage has since been remembered as the "Flower-Washing Brook," and that it has been immortalized in a mini-essay by the Late Ming poet and author of belles-lettres prose, Zhong Xing 鍾惺 (1574–1624). Giles, having worked assiduously during his docent training, has even memorized the lines that describe the stream: "There, turning westward, slender, lengthy, in graceful twists and turns; looking like a chain of circled rings, like a jade circle, like a girdle, like a roundel, like a hook; shining in its dark, deep green color like a mirror, like gemstone, like a dark green melon; and winding its way around and beneath the city wall, is the Flower-Washing Brook."[8] Listening to the bubbling murmur of the stream, Lynette and Giles feel like they have journeyed across time and space, not only to the classical Chinese authors, but also to the original Flower-Washing Brook half a world away.

Resuming their walk around the lake, they stroll across two bridges with names that contain rich layers of literary allusions. Delighted by the sight of numerous large fish under Yu Le Qiao 魚樂橋 (Bridge of the Joy of Fish), Lynette cites the famous conversation in the *Zhuangzi*, which starts from one's knowledge of fish ("You are not fish, so how do you know the joy of fish?") and leads to the profound topic of epistemology.[9] Farther to the west, at the bridge called Bu Yue 步月 (Strolling in the Moonlight), Giles associates the name with

---

7. For a discussion of the lotus and its virtues as a Buddhist symbol, see *Huayanjing tanxuanji* 華嚴經探玄記 [An Exploration of the Avatamsaka Sutra]. For the Chinese text see Fazang 法藏 (643–712), *Dafang guangfo huayanjing tanxuanji huiben* 大方廣佛華嚴經探玄記會本 (Taipei: Xinwenfeng chubanshe, 1983). See also Appendix A, no. 9.

8. For an English translation of Zhong Xing's text see my translation with annotations and an introduction, Yang Ye, *Vignettes from the Late Ming: A Hsiao-p'in Anthology* (Seattle: University of Washington Press, 1999), 63–64. See also Appendix A, no. 19.

9. This is from the chapter "Autumn Flood" 秋水 in the *Zhuangzi*. For the Chinese text, see Guo Xiang 郭象, *Zhuangzi zhu* 莊子注, *Siku quanshu* 四庫全書 ed., 6.19–20. See also Appendix A, no. 17.

Love for the Lotus Pavilion.

Pavilion of the Three Friends.

Freshwater Pavilion.

the great artist and poet Su Shi, more popularly remembered as Su Dongpo 蘇東坡, or Su the Eastern Slope, from his alias, Layman Buddhist of the Eastern Slope 東坡居士. Prompted by the sight of moonlight coming through the doorway, Su Dongpo impulsively visits a friend who is staying at a Buddhist temple. The two of them walk into the central courtyard, where the ground "resembled a body of water illuminated by moonlight" and the shadows of the bamboo and junipers looked like intertwining aquatic plants.[10]

After the long walk, Lynette is overjoyed at Giles's suggestion that they stop at the tea shop for a cup of fine tea while taking in the beautiful view of the lake and its surroundings through the elegant lattice windows. The somewhat pedantic Giles has done some research of his own on the age-old custom, and on their way to the tea shop he tells Lynette how tea drinking first became a bon ton in China during the Tang dynasty (618–907), as evidenced by *The Classic on Tea* 茶經 by Lu Yu 陸羽 (733–804), who has since become known as the "God of Tea" 茶神 or the "Sage of Tea" 茶聖. It became even more of a vogue, Giles continues, during the Northern Song dynasty (960–1126), notably with Emperor Huizong 宋徽宗 (1082–1135; who ruled 1100–1125), a tea connoisseur as well as a great artist.[11] According to tradition, the tea itself, the quality of the water, the method of cooking, and the utensils used for drinking are of almost equal importance. Lynette and Giles arrive at the tea shop and look up at the horizontal plaque identifying it: Huo Shui Xuan 活水軒 (Freshwater Pavilion). Lynette, searching in her mind for

10. For an English translation with annotations and an introduction of [*Jichengtianyeyou*] 記承天夜遊 from Su Dongpo's *Zhilin* 志林 [Forest of Jottings], "An Evening Stroll to the Temple that Receives the Heavenly" (1083), see Richard E. Strassberg, trans., *Inscribed Landscapes: Travel Writing from Imperial China* (Berkeley: University of California Press, 1994), 192–93. For the Chinese text, see Kong Fanli 孔凡禮, ed., *Su Shi wenji* 蘇軾文集 [Su Shi's Prose Writings], 6 vols., vol. 5 (Beijing: Zhonghua shuju, 1986), 71.2260. See also Appendix A, no. 18.
11. Emperor Huizong was the author of a book on tea, the *Daguan chalun* 大觀茶論 [Discourse on Tea from the Daguan Reign]. For this and Lu Yu's work, see the collection of twelve premodern works on tea, Lu Yu, *Chajing* [Classics on Tea] (Beijing: Zhongguo fangzhi chubanshe, 2006).

A painting of strolling in the moonlight: Shen Zongqian (Chinese, 1736–1820), *Su Dongpo's Evening Stroll to the Temple that Receives the Heavenly*, 1770. Nanjing Museum, Nanjing, People's Republic of China.

poems she memorized in childhood, promptly recalls the term *huo shui*, which literally means "living water," or "water with a life," from a poem on tea by none other than Su Dongpo. In the poem, he describes how he scoops up the crystal clear "living water" from the deep river, in order to make some tea on the spot, using a stove where a "living fire" 活火 is blazing.[12] At Giles's request, Lynette is glad to chant the poetic couplet inscribed on the vertical tablets at the entrance:

| *Xiao* | *shi* | *leng* | *quan* | *liu* | *zao* | *wei* | 小 石 冷 泉 留 早 味 |
| *Zi* | *ni* | *xin* | *pin* | *fan* | *chun* | *hua* | 紫 泥 新 品 泛 春 華 |

"The flavor of the early morning lingers in the cold spring water issued from the small rocks; spring blossoms waft from the new species steeped in a purple clay teapot." Lynette paraphrases the couplet, which was taken from another poem on tea by the poet's elder contemporary Mei Yaochen 梅堯臣 (1002–1060),[13] "How nice! I can hardly wait for a cup of the 'new species' inside there!" As Lynette and Giles enjoy their tea, it is time for us to leave them.

The Chinese conception of art and literature is of a vast inter-textual network formed throughout history that keeps expanding into the future. For example, Tao Yuanming's "Peach Blossom Spring" has generated not only entire collections of poems but also numerous landscape paintings.[14] The visitor's mental rumination is further enriched by the comparison between the Peach Blossom Spring and the Western concept of utopia.

Certainly, most visitors to Liu Fang Yuan are not as conversant with Chinese culture as Lynette and Giles, our fictitious visitors. However, through educational programs and written material such as the garden records collected in this book, visitors will understand, if partially, the iridescent cultural text behind each name. In due course, our Implied Visitor may play an active part in the continuous phenomenological game about names that, in their multiple layers of associations and allusions, may transcend both the visitor and the places they represent. By the same token, we may say that the Garden of Flowing Fragrance itself is inexhaustible in its aesthetic possibilities.

Yang Ye is Associate Professor of Chinese in the Department of Comparative Literature and Foreign Languages at University of California, Riverside.

12. The work is Su Dongpo's heptasyllabic regulated poem "Scooping Water from the River to Make Tea" 汲江煎茶. For the Chinese text see *Quan Song shi* 全宋詩 [Complete Song Poetry] (Beijing: Beijingdaxue chubanshe, 1993), 826.9567. For a somewhat free English translation of the poem ("Boiling Tea"), see Robert Payne, trans., *The White Pony: An Anthology of Chinese Poetry from the Earliest Times to the Present Day, Newly translated* (New York: J. Day Co., 1947), 269. See also Appendix A, no. 4.
13. The couplet is from Mei Yaochen's poem, "Following the Original Rime Pattern of Grand Councilor Du's Poem to Cao Junmo Thanking Him for Sending some Tea by Mail" 依韻和杜相公謝蔡君謨寄茶. For the Chinese text see *Quan Song shi* 全宋詩 [Complete Song Poetry], 253.3046. According to Emperor Huizong, the picking of tea leaves has to be done in early morning, before the sunrise. See Lu Yu, *Chajing* [Classics on Tea], 67.
14. The *Siku quanshu zongmu tiyao* 四庫全書總目提要 [The General Catalogue of the Four Treasuries of Books] observes that there were two anthologies of poems written on the topic of the Peach Blossom Spring, a single-volume collection published during the Song dynasty, and a three-volume one in the Ming dynasty. For the numerous paintings based on the subject see Richard M. Barnhart, *Peach Blossom Spring: Gardens and Flowers in Chinese Paintings* (New York: Metropolitan Museum of Art, 1983).

DECORATION *and* THEMES *in* LIU FANG YUAN

⊡⊡ T. June Li

The names of structures and sites in a traditional Chinese garden provide poetic inspiration for the visitor. As in a literati painting, the garden's composition of rocks and water is interspersed with inscriptions and subtle references to literature and art. Beautiful calligraphy, carved on wood placards or selected rocks, enhances themes chosen by the garden owner and offers a guide for contemplation. In Liu Fang Yuan, the names of the pavilions, bridges, lake, and streams provide a programmed cultural tour through notable structures and views in the garden.

Many of the architectural ornaments and landscape details in Liu Fang Yuan reinforce the themes of the garden. For example, the carved fish finials decorating the ends of the zigzag Bridge of the Joy of Fish, Yu Le Qiao 魚樂橋, recall the playful discussion between the Daoist Zhuangzi 莊子 and his friend the logician Huizi 惠子. This famous exchange centered on the enigma of whether it was possible for Zhuangzi to know that the fish in the river were happy, pitching the free-spirited Daoist ideas against the more pedantic arguments of logic.[1]

Because the conception of a Chinese garden at the Huntington was inspired by plants native to China, botanical motifs are prominent in Liu Fang Yuan, representing various threads of literary, cultural, and seasonal reference. For example, images of the chrysanthemum—a flower associated with the poet Tao Yuanming 陶淵明—are found throughout the garden in the form of roof-tile ends, which include triangular rain-drip and arched end-tiles. These symbolize Tao's idyllic garden, a simple refuge for an ideal life.[2] The motif was borrowed from

---

1. See Appendix A, no. 17.
2. See Yang Ye's essay on p. 56.

Roof-tile ends with chrysanthemum motif.

a pattern in the chrysanthemum volume of the *Mustard Seed Garden Manual of Painting* (*Jieziyuan Huapu* 芥子園畫譜), a book frequently consulted by painters and designers since its first publication in 1679.[3]

Another recurring floral pattern carved onto the wood beams and doors of several pavilions depicts the camellia. This design alludes not only to the Huntington's renowned collection of over 1,200 kinds of camellias but also to the plant's association with tea. In Chinese, the camellia is called *cha hua* 茶花, or tea flower, because the young leaves of *Camellia sinensis* are picked for tea. At the entrance to the tea shop—Freshwater Pavilion, or Huo Shui Xuan 活水軒—six different kinds of camellias are carved on the doors. Following an ancient practice, Southern California artist Liang Peifang 梁北方 drew these camellia patterns for master carvers in Suzhou to work from.

The camellia theme is echoed in the nearby tea house, called Hall of the Jade Camellia, or Yu Ming Tang 玉茗堂, and named after the residence of famous playwright Tang Xianzu 湯顯祖 (1550–1616), author of the acclaimed play *Peony Pavilion*. Tang is thought to have invoked the *yuming* flower, a white

Design of chrysanthemum in the *Mustard Seed Garden Manual of Painting*.

Carved camellia on a door panel of the Freshwater Pavilion.

---

3. This design is from *Jieziyuan Huapu* 芥子園畫譜 (Taipei: Huazheng shuju 華正書局, 1979), vol. 2, pp. 213, 217.

Painting of camellia by artist Liang Peifang.

Feng Dayou (Chinese, twelfth century, Song dynasty), *Lotuses in the Wind at T'aiye*, undated. Album leaf, ink and color on silk; 23.8 x 25.1 cm. National Palace Museum, Taipei, Taiwan, Republic of China.

Love for the Lotus Pavilion.

Eight carved wood panels of Suzhou gardens in Love for the Lotus Pavilion.

camellia, because it represented purity and naturalness.[4] Early writers declared its beauty to be without rival, associating the exquisite flower with the virtues of a high-minded individual.

In Liu Fang Yuan, stems of camellia blossoms and buds are carved onto the wood beams of the tea house, the tea shop, and the pavilion associated with the lotus. The Love for the Lotus Pavilion, or Ai Lian Xie 愛蓮榭, is an elegant open building that looks out over the Pond of Reflected Greenery, Bi Zhao Tang 碧照塘. Here, "greenery" refers to the profusion of lotus leaves that appear to float and hover over the water during the summer months, accompanied by pristine blossoms of white and pink. Because the lotus rises out of mud, it has been a symbol of simplicity and purity for centuries. The pavilion's name underscores this reference by alluding to Zhou Dunyi's 周敦頤 famous eleventh-century essay "Ai Lian Shuo" 愛蓮說, which places the lotus first among flowers.[5]

Framed by delicate traceries, the openings of Ai Lian Xie provide glimpses into a refined interior. Here, twelve yellow cypress panels on the pond side of the pavilion are carved front and back with plum blossoms, bamboo, lotus, orchid, chrysanthemum, and pine. At the back of the pavilion, a carved screen of *nanmu* 楠木, from the laurel family, reveals intricate scenes of eight famous gardens in Suzhou.[6]

A hexagonal, double-storied structure further along the lake is named the Pavilion of the Three Friends, or San You Ge 三友閣. It has surrounding views of nearby pines, with distant

---

4. During the Song dynasty, the *yuming* flower was celebrated in Linchuan 臨川, Jiangxi Province (*Linchuan fuzhi* 臨川府誌). The Song calligrapher Huang Tingjian 黃庭堅 (1045–1105) composed a prose poem called *Baishancha Fu* 白山茶賦 [Rhapsody on the White Camellia]. See Appendix A, no. 5.

5. See Yang Ye's essay on p. 58 and Appendix A, no. 9.

6. The eight gardens represented are, from right to left: Spirit-Cliff Hill (Lingyan shan) 靈岩山, Cold Mountain Temple (Hanshan si) 寒山寺, Blue Wave Pavilion (Canglang ting) 滄浪亭, Garden for Lingering (Liu Yuan) 留園, the Artless Administrator's Garden (Zhuozheng Yuan) 拙政園, Tiger Hill (Huqiu) 虎丘, Lion Grove (Shizilin) 獅子林, and Master of the Nets Garden (Wangshi Yuan) 網師園.

Zhao Mengjian (Chinese, 1199–1264), *Three Friends of the Cold Season*, undated. Album leaf, ink on paper, 32.2 x 53.4 cm. National Palace Museum, Taipei, Taiwan, Republic of China.

Pavilion of the Three Friends.

Plaque in the Pavilion of the Three Friends.

"Listening to the Pines" inscription.

bamboo and plum trees to the north. Its circular ceiling also bears carved motifs of these three plants, revered as the "three friends of the cold season," or *suihan san you* 歲寒三友. They share the characteristic of thriving even amid the cold. In northern China, the leafless plum blooms in early spring despite ice and snow, and the bamboo and pine are evergreens. These three have come to represent courage and tenacity against adversity, and they are celebrated in Chinese art, literature, and gardens. To accompany this theme of survival in cold weather, the latticework on the openings just under the ceiling of this pavilion shows the traditional "broken ice" pattern.

The bridge called Listening to the Pines, or Ting Song 聽松, affords an unsurpassed view of a meandering stream lined with peach trees, which appears to emerge from the foothills of the distant San Gabriel Mountains. As the water tumbles softly over rocks, several layered literary references are evoked. This is the Flower Washing Brook, or Huan Hua Xi 浣花溪, which takes its name from the stream-side cottage of the beloved eighth-century poet Du Fu 杜甫.[7] The banks of the Flower Washing Brook are planted with spring-blossoming peach trees that recall Tao Yuanming's story "Peach Blossom Spring," in which a fisherman follows a peach blossom–lined spring to a mountain cave that leads to a hidden utopian world.[8] The winding stream also recalls the gathering of poets at the Orchid Pavilion in Shaoxing 紹興 in 353, when wine cups were floated down the stream as poems were written.

7. See Yang Ye's account on p. 58. See also Appendix A, no. 19.
8. See Yang Ye's account on p. 56 and Appendix A, no. 2.

Wang Xizhi 王羲之 (303–361)—one of China's greatest calligraphers—wrote about the occasion in his "Preface to the Poems Composed at the Orchid Pavilion" (Lanting Xu 蘭亭序). His much-emulated calligraphy is treasured as the finest example of running script, which epitomizes self-expression.

These are just some of the many cultural references of Liu Fang Yuan. Everywhere the visitor turns, plantings, decorations, calligraphy, and carefully crafted views integrate centuries of Chinese refinement.

Even features beyond the garden's borders are brought into play. Look north, and the San Gabriel Mountains form a painterly backdrop. Look south from the Studio of Pure Scents, or Qing Fen Zhai 清芬齋, over the Cascade of Resonant Bamboo, or Zhu Yun Quan 竹韻泉, and the stream below flows by a thatched structure, the Pavilion for Washing Away Thoughts, Di Lü Ting 滌慮亭. Its rustic roof contrasts with the surrounding lushness of the camellia-lined canyon to create yet another composition in the painting that is Liu Fang Yuan.

T. June Li is the Curator of Liu Fang Yuan.

Fan Yi (Chinese, active ca. 1658–71, Qing dynasty), *Purification at the Orchid Pavilion*, detail, 1671. Handscroll, ink and color on silk; 28.1 x 392.8 cm. © The Cleveland Museum of Art, Gift of Mrs. Wai–kam Ho and the Womens Council of The Cleveland Museum of Art 1977.47.

Evergreens in Liu Fang Yuan.

CHINESE PLANTS *and* LIU FANG YUAN:

A BOTANICAL HERITAGE

James Folsom

Had Western gardens never been enriched with plants from China, they would look quite different. Imagine the landscape and orchards of California without peaches, apricots, and oranges—or flower gardens without lilacs or forsythia, peonies or chrysanthemums, wisteria or spiraea. Picture rows of roses that bloom only for a brief spell in late spring.

One of many beautiful selections of *Hibiscus rosa-sinensis*.

If the beauties and pleasures of these and hundreds of other plants from China were unknown today, imagine the delight each new plant would bring with its arrival. The peach, for example, is one of the most useful and easily propagated of Chinese plants. This delicious relative of the plum and cherry made its way to the Western world very early—so early and through such belabored trade routes that its origins became obscured. Thus European botanists gave it the name *Prunus persica*, guessing at an exotic origin in the Levant. Other useful and economically important plants, such as *Citrus sinensis*, the sweet orange, were not known to Westerners until the first trade vessels made direct contact with Asia in 1487. Most ornamental plants of Chinese origin did not appear in the West until well after direct trade began between Asia and Europe in the mid-seventeenth century.[1]

---

1. See Peter Valder, *The Garden Plants of China* (Portland, Ore.: Timber Press, 1999), esp. 63–69.

Rhododendron 'Forsterianum' in springtime bloom at the east entrance to Liu Fang Yuan.

Today, we romanticize intrepid explorers who trek the wilds of an exotic land, seek new and exciting plants, and return with specimens and seeds for study and cultivation. This did happen in China, but it is not at all the history behind the Chinese plants that now populate gardens and groves. Early Western explorers found their treasures not in the wilds but in the gardens and nurseries that had long been part of Chinese culture. Centuries before the arrival of Western travelers, when Europe was yet in its Dark Ages and barely making a dent in the practice of gardening, nurseries flourished in China, brimming with special forms of the most wonderful plants, forms that reflected generations of producing and selecting. The gardens of China were filled with such plants, their refinement based on both aesthetic and practical criteria.

These Chinese plants were destined to grow well in the gardens of Europe and North America because they bore crucial affinities to plants those continents already possessed. The North Temperate climate of Asia resembles that experienced by the plants of Europe and North America, so the growing conditions are similar in all three places. Moreover, were it not for the geological creep known as continental drift, the gradual, steady movement of continents away from one another, Asia, North America, and Europe would yet be a single giant landmass, as they were in the greatly distant past, and the North Temperate flora of these three continents would have remained intact. Camellias, dogwoods, roses, lilies, trilliums,

Terraced *penjing* display at Tiger Hill, in Suzhou.

Paeonia suffruticosa 'Qing Lo'.

Red-flowered tree peony.

and azaleas would never have fallen victim to the vagaries of distance and political boundaries. Thus, an ancient heritage of plants, a several-hundred-million-year-old relationship that we have come to understand only during the last century, provides the botanical larder for today's gardens.

Asia inherited the richest portion of the great North Temperate flora because its landmass was larger and its climate change not as dramatic, meaning that greater diversity survived over the eons. So Chinese gardeners not only developed their craft much earlier but also had more to work with in the first place. In practical terms, what does this heritage say about traditional Chinese gardens several centuries ago, or even today? What does this biological and horticultural development mean in the Huntington's Liu Fang Yuan?

PLANTS IN A CHINESE GARDEN

Centuries before Western gardeners began experimenting with native European plants for ornamental use, Chinese gardeners had scoured their country for the most beautiful and exciting as well as the most cultivatable of native flora. That dedication played out across the wider region, from Xi'an to Beijing to Suzhou into what is Hong Kong today. Gardeners studied and selected plants from a wide range of habitats, cold to warm, wet to dry. Among the smaller, herbaceous plants, the spring-flowering peonies, the summer-blooming daylilies with orange and yellow flowers, and the autumn-flowering chrysanthemums were domesticated very early and commonly used in gardens. Chinese horticulturists developed countless forms, richly floriferous and so highly selected as to nearly appear to be separate species from their wild ancestors. These plants were greatly admired and appreciated, as any student of Chinese art and literature can attest.

Forsythia suspensa.

Though herbaceous plants provide welcome flowers, and can fill pots or cover small areas, Chinese gardens depend more heavily on a wonderful selection of woody plants for their structure. Shrubs were the mainstay of ancient Chinese landscapes, including many that are valued for their form and greenery, such as nandina, appreciated for its resemblance to bamboo, and juniper, an evergreen that tolerates pruning so well that it lends itself to interesting shapes and branching.

Many woody plants were loved, of course, for their flowers as well as their evergreen foliage. Azaleas were prized for their adaptability to both garden plantings and containers. Camellias, treasured for their many red, white, and pink flowers (some of which resembled the prized peonies), were also appreciated for their young leaves, which could be harvested for tea, especially the leaves of *Camellia sinensis*. Chinese gardeners have long cherished plants that produce beautiful fragrances. Some of the world's most highly regarded fragrant shrubs were critical components of early Chinese gardens, such as the tea olive (*Osmanthus fragrans*), the gardenias, and the trailing jasmines.

Among the many shrubs are numerous important deciduous plants known from early Chinese gardens. Lilacs come quickly to mind for their abundant flowers and wonderful fragrance. Another plant, not fragrant, but spectacularly timely, is the forsythia, which flowers soon after Chinese New Year with abundant showers of golden flowers that promise a spring of garden wealth.

Podocarpus with prayer ribbons at Buddhist temple in Shanghai.

Pink flowering peach and snowball viburnum.

Prunus mume, flowering on a frosty January morning.

Deciduous shrubs and small trees in the rose family are particularly significant contributions from Chinese horticulture. Wide-ranging forms of peaches, plums, apricots, and quinces comprise one of the greatest green legacies, all due to the dedication of early Chinese gardeners. Peaches, both fruiting and sterile forms, are woven into Chinese culture from ancient times, and were present anywhere the trees could be cultivated.[2] This was also true of plums and apricots. However, the kind known as *mei hua* (*Prunus mume*) is particularly revered for its capacity to bloom in winter. The audacity to flower during cold, harsh weather brings the *mei hua* its honor as one of the "three friends of the cold season"—the other two being pine and bamboo, which grace the landscape with stem and leaf alone.[3]

2. See the legend of Peach Blossom Spring in Appendix A, no. 2.
3. See T. June Li's essay on p. 69.

Michelia alba.

Trachycarpus fortunei, Chinese windmill palm, in the Huntington's Palm Garden, the tallest of the palms native to Chinese landscapes.

Other trees vary widely in impact from region to region in China. In historical gardens in northern regions, honor was given to the pines for their beauty and evergreen nature; to the curious *Firmiana*; to *Sophora*, appreciated as the scholar tree; to the maples for their delicate, beautifully colored foliage and muscular stem shapes; to the generously flowering magnolias; and to the productive plants—persimmon, mulberry, and ginkgo.

For centuries, tropical and subtropical plants have been grown in Chinese gardens wherever possible, even if in containers and requiring protection during the winter. Kumquats have long been known as far north as Beijing, and sweet oranges were developed in South China. The Chinese windmill palm, hardier than almost any other, appears in ancient scroll paintings as a long-standing feature of gardens throughout much of China. Chinese gardens in more tropical zones, such as Taiwan and Hong Kong, show a very different plant palette. The fragrant magnolia relative *Michelia alba* is commonly grown in these zones, and the narrow-petaled white flowers are offered for sale as amulets throughout southern China.

And anyone who has visited Hong Kong knows of the famous orchid tree, a spectacular *Bauhinia blakeana* that serves as the region's emblem and is now cultivated throughout the tropics. The plant originated from a single tree, protected through its cultivation in the southern city of Guangzhou and not known from any wild forms.

Some exotics occur over a wide range, most particularly the pomegranate (a shrub) and the banana (an overblown herb), which have long-standing presence in China, introduced more than a millennium ago. The pomegranate, native to the Mediterranean, reflects ancient trade relationships, and in China symbolizes multiple offspring, just as it does in its native land. Bananas, depicted so frequently in courtyard pots, were native to India. Revered for their delicious fruit and handsome leaves, they have long been associated with the Chinese scholar.

But the garden scene in China is not static: a visitor to China today would also find gardens boasting many significant plants that were brought into cultivation over the past century. The Southern magnolia (in China called *hehua yulan* 荷花玉蘭, or lotus-flower magnolia), native to southeastern North America, has become widely used in gardens and along the streets of Shanghai and Suzhou, where the temperature, humidity, and rainfall are near-perfect duplicates of those in its native range. The streets of Shanghai are also lined with the London plane, a hybrid *Platanus* found in the city's gardens and parks. Even native Chinese plants that were not part of ancient horticulture have found new roles. One of the most common trees in the gardens of Suzhou and Shanghai is the lovely dawn redwood—a deciduous conifer known from one small population in China that was not available for horticulture until 1948.

Plantains, flourishing in midsummer in the courtyard.

PLANTS IN LIU FANG YUAN

Not all plants thrive at the Huntington. The palette of plants best suited for Liu Fang Yuan excludes some splendid examples, either because the temperatures in Southern California are too cold, or more often, not cold enough. In other cases, the rainfall and humidity are simply too low here.

Plane trees lining the streets of Shanghai's French Concession zone.

Bamboo in a Suzhou garden.

Tufts of lily turfs in a garden in Suzhou.

Generally, Southern California's climate most closely approximates that of Suzhou, and the plants most commonly used in that garden city indicate the choices that might best grow at the Huntington. Even though the near-subtropical climate and summer dry season of Southern California pose numerous challenges, the garden includes the most important plants one would see in Suzhou, plants that have been featured in that city's gardens for hundreds of years. The architectural structures of Liu Fang Yuan set these plants in a landscape and cultural context that reflects their significance and value.

Certain plants are important to the garden because of their particular histories and symbolic meanings, others because they perform particularly well here. The most mature and beautiful trees in the garden are native California oaks, original to the site and purposely incorporated into the garden's design in reverence to their age and beauty. The selection of plants at the center of the garden is meant to represent what a visitor to one of the great Suzhou classical gardens would encounter, with willows and elms forming the canopy, camellias and nandinas providing structure, and smaller shrubbery embracing the rockeries and edges. In the surrounding woodlands, a visitor to Liu Fang Yuan comes upon a broader representation of Chinese flora, along with their nearest relatives (called vicariads by botanists) from across the historical North Temperate flora—just as a visitor to China would encounter a broader spectrum of the great Chinese flora by leaving the built garden for the countryside. Notable

Golden canopy of ginkgo in autumn.

Fall color along the Great Wall, north of Beijing.

examples include the magnolias, sweetgums, catalpas, dogwoods, redbuds, plums, oaks, elms, and chestnuts.

Several themes can be discovered in the greenery. Liu Fang Yuan is the only truly seasonal garden at the Huntington, emphasizing and symbolizing the progression of winter, spring, summer, and autumn. As mentioned earlier, the "three friends of the cold season"—*mei hua*, pine, and bamboo—play a prominent role in the landscape. While so many trees and shrubs in the garden form gnarly, bare silhouettes, the pine and bamboo are resilient and green, and the beautiful white and pink blossoms of *mei hua* open, perfect even in morning frost. Spring unfolds from March through May, a play of peach, plum, forsythia, and peonies amid the new green of pendulous willow branches and the burgundy of emerging maple leaves. Summer progresses toward the heat of August—but not without June's gift of lotus leaves rising to hover above the water, punctuated by the most elegant and pristine lotus blossoms, symbolic of purity and transcendence—or without the melon and orchid colors of crape myrtle. The shade of oaks, willows, and elms is welcome through the dry and torrid days of late summer, with shortening days bearing the promise of cooler weather and the autumn color of chrysanthemums, as well as fall foliage, with the gold of ginkgo, the bronze of sweet gum, and the fire of pistache.

The visitor experiences more than the visual realm, for the garden's name hints at rich fragrance. With winter rains, the resinous aroma of pine and juniper fills the garden, with heady plumes of wax plum and the fragrant bush honeysuckle we call "kiss me at the gate" evident amid drifts of narcissus and early flowering bulbs along pathways. Flowering fruit trees, oranges, and lilac highlight spring, permeated with the fruitiness of wisteria flowers. Summer is heavy with gardenia, and lightly perfumed with michelia. Fall ushers in the late-season flushes of bloom from the white tea olive and the peachy fragrance of the lovely golden osmanthus.

More important, woody and herbaceous plants alike shelter and reveal pavilions and roofs, and play against wall, water, and sky to bring nature and life to the structures. Twisting branches of native California live oak frame the canopy; romantic drapings of willow and jasmine curtain the lake. Bold plantains and bamboo contrast with smooth whitewashed walls. Tufts of mondo and lacy mounds of maple and pine populate the ground plane and merge with rockery. Dark and pale, coarse and fine—the layering and depth of plantings create new vistas with every turn of the path, even at each fresh glance. The garden becomes a discovery, each moment a unique experience, suddenly a memory, as the plants pursue their cycles of growth and development.

James Folsom is the Marge and Sherm Telleen Director of the Botanical Gardens.

Racemes of fragrant wisteria, draped over walkways in the Japanese Garden.

Spring-flowering Taiwan cherry, *Prunus taiwaniana*, viewed from the Studio of Pure Scents in Liu Fang Yuan.

Flowering peach along the stream flowing into the Japanese Garden.

Flowering peach in the Liu Fang Yuan woodland.

Prunus campanulata, Taiwan flowering cherry.

A GARDEN GLOSSARY FOR LIU FANG YUAN*

Acer

MAPLE
楓 *feng*

One could not have a Chinese garden without the tracery of beautifully branching maples. These small trees, with their hand-shaped leaves and helicopter fruits, bring movement and change, from wintry silhouettes of delicate branches, to springtime emergence of chartreuse and red-tipped leaves and flowers, to summer fullness and fall color.

Bambusa spp.

BAMBOO
桂竹 *guizhu*

Bamboos are in fact spectacular grasses that make two kinds of stems. Rhizomes creep along or under the earth, eventually producing shoots that elongate to become tall canes that are called culms. Golden bamboo and black bamboo are among the more famous of the running types, sending their underground rhizomes long distances before the tips turn up to make shoots. The young, tender shoots of many bamboos are an important food source, and the mature, woody culms are important for construction.

Calocedrus decurrens

CALIFORNIA INCENSE CEDAR
北美翠柏 *beimei cuibai*

A California relative of China's important junipers and cypresses, incense cedar grows natively in the San Gabriel Mountains and can be seen planted along streets and gardens throughout the area. An ancient grove in the Huntington, with handsome red-brown ropy and twisted bark, gives special character to the eastern entrance of Liu Fang Yuan. The fine clear wood of incense cedar has many uses but is best known for its historic utility in the manufacture of pencils.

*Plants are listed alphabetically by botanical name.

Camellia reticulata

CAMELLIA

南山茶 *nan shancha*

Camellias are core plantings for Liu Fang Yuan, as they are crucial components for both Suzhou gardens and the Huntington, which is home to the largest collection of these plants in North America. The most common camellias in Liu Fang Yuan are the reticulatas and the japonicas, which have flowers in the white to pink and red color ranges and bloom during our winter.

Camellia sinensis

TEA

茶樹 *chashu*

One of the plants most closely associated with China is a small-leaved, small-flowered camellia that is grown for its leaves, which are the source of tea. Harvested while they are yet tender and rust-colored, the leaves can be quickly dried to make green teas or specially processed to make the many black teas. Visitors will find plants of *Camellia sinensis* in the Plantain Court.

Chaenomeles japonica

FLOWERING QUINCE

日本木瓜 *riben mugua*

Flowering early in the year, and always at its peak over Chinese New Year, the shrubby quince is appreciated both for floral color and for use in flower arrangements. Like its relatives, apples and roses, the quince bears flowers with five petals and produces useful fruit.

Chimonanthus praecox

WINTERSWEET

臘梅 *lamei*

On cool, moist days in winter, the fragrance of *Chimonanthus* drifts in extended plumes throughout a garden, causing visitors to wonder what might be the source. It is found in the small, white or yellow, waxy and diaphanous flowers produced closely along the bare branches of the wintersweet. Remembering that the attractiveness of flowers is meant for pollinators, and is only an incidental gift to humans, we should not be surprised that flowers of powerful fragrance, such as wintersweet, may not be very showy—aroma alone may suffice for reproductive success.

CHINESE FRINGE TREE

流蘇 *liusu*

With loose clusters of delicate, long-petaled white flowers, the Chinese fringe tree makes an airy, cloud-like show in mid-spring, just as its large, yellow-green leaves begin to develop. With dense, shrubby branching, this deciduous tree can develop very handsome trunks and stems, giving beautiful character to its winter silhouette. A close relative of osmanthus, the fringe tree makes a great show of flowers but lacks the drifting fragrance.

Chionanthus retusus

CHRYSANTHEMUM

菊花 *juhua*

Among the more familiar of the daisies, chrysanthemums send up new shoots each spring that come into flower in autumn. Over the centuries, Chinese horticulturists selected hundreds of forms in colors ranging from whites and yellows to pinks and bronzes. They are often displayed as pot specimens that have been highly trained over the growing season.

Chrysanthemum ×morifolium

CAMPHOR

樟樹 *zhangshu*

Among the most common and useful trees for Southern California landscapes, China's camphor tree is easily recognized by its finely ridged bark, open, rounded crown, and small, shimmering chartreuse to green leaves. The best giveaway to identification is the presence, throughout the year, of a few red-orange leaves scattered throughout the canopy. A near relative of cinnamon and a distant relative of Europe's bay laurel and America's avocado, camphor has this group's characteristic green stems with their spicy aroma.

Cinnamomum camphora

KUMQUAT
BUDDHA'S HAND CITRON
金橘 *jinjü*
佛手柑 *foshou gan*

Several of the world's most important citrus trees are native to China, where they have been cultivated and valued for centuries. Kumquats and the Buddha's Hand citron are common container plants for courtyards, where they provide attractive color and fragrant fruit. Sweet oranges, which made Southern California an agricultural empire, are also native to Indochina. Visitors can see eight acres of the important juice-producing 'Valencia' orange in groves east of the Botanical Center.

Fortunella margarita

Citrus medica

SAGO PALM
蘇鐵 *sutie*

The palm-like sagos, which are native to the subtropical coast of China and southern Japan, have long been popular courtyard plants in China because of their exotic, evergreen formality, as well as their longevity and the ease with which they can be cultivated in containers. These attributes have also made them important garden plants in warmer climates around the world. Even more ancient than pine trees, cycads are among the oldest of seed-bearing plants, producing male and female cones on separate individuals.

Cycas revoluta

CYMBIDIUM
建蘭 *jianlan*

Delicate and modest in color and size, cymbidiums are among the orchids favored in Chinese gardens, celebrated for their beautifully arching foliage and pleasantly perfumed flowers. They are emblematic of spring and of scholarship.

Cymbidium ensifolium

CHINESE PARASOL TREE, PHOENIX TREE

梧桐 *wutong*

Called the Chinese parasol tree, *Firmiana* is a most peculiar kind of plant—with large leaves and coarse, stiff branches that form umbrella-like tiers along a green bole. Deciduous in the winter, the phoenix tree does indeed look to be the perfect perch for a propitious and mythical bird.

Firmiana simplex

FORSYTHIA

金鐘花 *jinzhonghua*

Among China's great contributions to gardens of the midwest and northeast United States, forsythia is also an appealing garden plant here in Southern California. Flowering a beautiful golden yellow with the New Year, forsythia brings good fortune to the Flower Washing Brook.

Forsythia viridissima

GARDENIA

栀子 *zhizi*

A Chinese representative of the coffee family, gardenia has long been prized and selected for the richly floral fragrance of its soft, white blossoms. Many forms are available for gardeners, ranging from larger-leaved shrubs to compact, small-leaved cultivars—some with variegated foliage. The more popular garden varieties have fully double flowers. Gardenias are featured at the main entrance of Liu Fang Yuan, where they perfume the air over many months of the year.

Gardenia jasminoides

GINKGO

銀杏, 白果, 鴨掌樹 *yinxing, baiguo, yazhangshu*

The ginkgo is not a flowering plant but a conifer relative, producing its seed on short stems of female trees and its pollen in cones on separate male plants. Most easily recognized by its fan-shaped leaves, ginkgo is known also for its knobby stems and golden yellow fall color. Not found in large natural populations, ginkgo would probably be extinct today but for its preservation in Chinese temple compounds.

Ginkgo biloba

DAYLILY
黃花菜, 萱草 *huanghuacai, xuancao*

Among the daylilies, all of which are native to Asia, the best-known species are the yellow *Hemerocallis lilio-asphodelus* and the tawny orange *Hemerocallis fulva*, both of which have long been common in Chinese gardens and lore. Dried buds of daylilies, called golden needles, are used in Chinese cooking, and plants of *xuan* in the garden are said to bring memory and honor to one's mother. Thick-rooted perennial herbs, daylilies are easy to cultivate and have become one of North America's most popular garden plants, yielding thousands of cultivars at the hands of backyard hybridizers.

Hemerocallis fulva

HIBISCUS
朱槿 木芙蓉, 拒霜花 *zhujin mufurong, jushuanghua*

This colorful member of the cotton family, linked in our minds to Hawaii and the South Sea Islands, is a tropical Asian vagabond that was transported to temperate regions of China, where it became a popular garden plant well before other travelers planted it around the world. Its bold flowers and mop of stamens, short-lived like those of its relatives, each last only a single day.

Hibiscus rosa-sinensis

Hibiscus mutabilis

PRIMROSE JASMINE
雲南黃素馨 *yunnan huang suxin*

Draping over stonework along the margin of ponds and streams in Suzhou gardens, the primrose jasmine softens and unites the hardscape while providing a nearly year-round sprinkling of golden yellow flowers. It performs the same magic at Liu Fang Yuan.

Jasminum mesnyi

CHINESE JUNIPER

圓柏 *yuanbai*

From shrub to tree, Chinese juniper is grown in hundreds of forms, with foliage in shades of green to silver and textures ranging from smooth to spiny. Pollen and seed are produced in simple cones, but since junipers are dioecious they do not form on the same plants. Only the female plants yield blue-gray "berries" that carry the seed.

Juniperus chinensis

GOLDEN RAIN TREE

欒樹 *luanshu*

Native to China and Korea, *luan* has ancient status in cultivation, known as one of the five memorial trees as long as 3,000 years ago. The golden yellow flowers, which give it the English name of golden rain tree, mature into large masses of colorful, papery fruit in advance of fall, when the entire tree goes deciduous.

Koelreuteria paniculata

CRAPE MYRTLE

紫薇, 百日紅 *ziwei, bairihong*

The most prominent summer-flowering tree in the garden is crape myrtle, with its large clusters of flowers ranging from lavenders and reds to watermelon pinks to whites. Displayed against a background of light green leaves, with a skeleton of muscular white-barked trunks and stems, the showy flowers give this patio-sized tree great seasonal presence in the landscape. Native to East Asia, crape myrtle has long been enjoyed in Chinese gardens from Beijing to Shanghai, and has been planted in Western gardens since Robert Fortune sent material to England in 1759.

Lagerstroemia indica

CHINESE PRIVET
女貞 *nüzhen*

The Chinese privets are hardy plants that produce shrubby branches of lovely, simple green foliage that tolerate pruning and clipping, making them wonderful for hedging, and even as small shade trees in Southern California gardens. Just like their other relatives in the olive family, privets bear leaves in pairs and produce clusters of small white flowers at the ends of their branches, making quite a show in early to mid-summer. When they are not sheared but allowed to grow more naturally, the flowers mature as clusters of purple berries in late summer.

Ligustrum lucidum

SWEETGUM
北美楓香樹 *beimei fengxiangshu*

Two kinds of sweetgum can be found in Liu Fang Yuan, the Asian *Liquidambar formosana* and its near relative *Liquidambar styraciflua*, native to North America. Both bear lobed leaves, similar in appearance to those of maple. Unlike maple, they produce seed in woody, spiked fruiting balls that can cover the ground in early winter. Our native *L. styraciflua* produces the most spectacular fall color.

Liquidambar styraciflua

MAGNOLIA
玉蘭 *yulan*

Magnolias are among the most ancient of flowering trees, showing the earliest kinds of adaptation to insect pollination. This lineage is part of the broader group of plants characterizing the North Temperate flora. The closest relatives of Asian magnolias are native to the eastern United States. Flowers of these trees are composed of many showy and simple parts, with multiple tepals, stamens, and pistils arranged in a tight spiral.

Magnolia denudata

DAWN REDWOOD
水杉 *shuishan*

Known by Western scientists from fossils before they learned that living examples had existed in cultivation for centuries in China, the dawn redwood was christened a living fossil when its seed were distributed by Arnold Arboretum to gardens around the world in 1948. Young plants form a small grove by the Flower Washing Brook, but visitors can examine large trees in the lily ponds garden that Huntington staff grew from that first seed distribution.

Metasequoia glyptostroboides

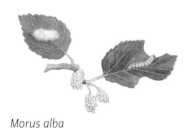

Michelia figo

BANANA SHRUB
含笑 *hanxiao*

Banana shrub is really a kind of magnolia, but unlike the showier kinds it produces small, pale yellow flowers. The blossoms make up in fragrance what they lack in size, however, producing a rich aroma reminiscent of ripe bananas. An example can be seen in the Plantain Court.

Morus alba

WHITE MULBERRY
桑 *sang*

The garden would not be complete without mulberry, a tree that has influenced Chinese culture and industry as the food source for domesticated silkworms. A handsome mulberry provides shade on the slope above the Listening to the Pines bridge, each spring producing a new crop of soft, fuzzy, heart-shaped leaves. The nearest relatives of mulberry at the Huntington, similar in leaf and branching, are the cultivated fig tree and *Broussonetia papyrifera*, the paper mulberry, which makes thin, platy bark used for manufacturing paper.

BANANA, PLANTAIN
香蕉 *xiangjiao*

Native to East Asia, the plantains (also called bananas) are not just among the world's most wonderful tropical fruits, but have also taken on special significance in China, where the exotic presence of plantains in courtyards is associated with the scholar. Moreover, they exemplify a historic love of plants and respect for those that yield food and useful products. People sometimes call them trees, but by any botanical standard plantains are more comparable structurally to the bamboos—spreading through clustering, creeping rhizomatous stems that shoot up to form upright leafy stems that eventually flower and fruit.

Musa ×paradisiaca

HEAVENLY BAMBOO, NANDINA
南天竹 *nan tianzhu*

Not at all a bamboo, nandina produces cane-like stems bearing large, branch-like leaves. What appears to be a single leaf, like the leaf of a bamboo, is therefore really a leaf segment, or leaflet. Each spring a cluster of small white flowers is produced, maturing to become a cluster of red fruit that remains showy through the year. A special form with golden colored fruit can be found along the southern edge of the Plantain Court.

Nandina domestica

NARCISSUS

水仙 *shuixian*

Narcissus are wonderful for celebrating the New Year because the bulbs can easily be stored and transported, and because they can be planted in decorative pots of gravel and water where they are forced into flower just in time for the annual festivities. Their white and gold flowers bring cheerful symbolism to the season. Though not native to China, narcissus bulbs were brought to cultivation there through trade routes a thousand years ago, and the plants have now naturalized in many areas.

Narcissus tazetta subsp. *tazetta*

LOTUS

荷花 *hehua*

Famous for its beauty, utility, and symbolism, lotus is at the center of the garden. Emblematic of summer, lotus goes dormant in autumn, emerging only as water temperatures rise in late spring. The first leaves to appear are floating, like those of the related water lily, but plate-like summer leaves rise high above the water surface, creating a greenness where there had been water surface. Punctuating the low canopy are the plant's large, star-like flowers, which mature into characteristic flat-topped pods.

Nelumbo nucifera

MONDO GRASS

沿階草, 麥冬 *yanjiecao, maidong*

So important for groundcover and small accents because of their graceful, handsome foliage, the evergreen mondo grasses and lily turfs seldom strike visitors as related to lilies. It is only on close examination that we see the similarities of flower and fruit. Some of the larger mondos actually do produce striking blue fruit, but they are grown mainly for their grassy, green texture.

Ophiopogon japonicus

SWEET OSMANTHUS, TEA OLIVE

木犀, 桂花 *muxi, guihua*

The different kinds of osmanthus are among the most nondescript of evergreen shrubs—bushy, with simple leaves and small flowers. However, when flowers have such beautiful fragrance, anything more would be ostentatious. The common name, "tea olive," reflects both their historical use as companion plants to camellias and their biological relationship to other members of the olive family. Two kinds of tea olive, the white-flowered *Osmanthus fragrans* and the peachy-golden *O. fragrans* f. *aurantiacus*, are common in Liu Fang Yuan.

Osmanthus fragrans

Paeonia suffruticosa

Paulownia tomentosa

Pinus thunbergii, Pinus spp.

Pistacia chinensis

TREE PEONY, MOUTAN

牡丹 *mudan*

A difficult plant for the gardens of Southern California, the peony is still worth every bit of horticultural effort, both for the sumptuous beauty of its over-blown flowers and for the wealth of symbolism peonies have for Chinese horticulture. Of the two main kinds, the herbaceous (with leaves and stems that die to the ground each year) and the tree type (with stems that remain as short trunks), the tree peonies are somewhat more successful in our gardens. Many other kinds of plants, such as certain camellias and roses, are prized for flowers that resemble those of peonies.

EMPRESS TREE, PRINCESS TREE

毛泡桐, 泡桐 *mao paotong, paotong*

Valued as a useful timber tree, paulownia was historically planted in Chinese gardens to mark the birth of a daughter, as a symbol of the wood required for her future dowry wardrobes. Visitors will easily discern the coarsely branched tree with foot-long heart-shaped leaves, especially in spring, when it is covered with massive heads of large, tubular, pale purple flowers.

BLACK PINE

黑松 *heisong*

Producing their seed in cones, not in flowers, pines are quintessential conifers—with needles and scales instead of typical broad leaves. The smaller, trained pines in the garden are the Asian *Pinus thunbergii*. The towering pine forest to the west and north is rich with *P. torreyana* from Southern California, *P. halepensis* of Europe, and *P. canariensis*, native to the Canary Islands—trees that have been on this site for over seventy years and are common elements in the Southern California landscape.

CHINESE PISTACHE

黃連木 *huanglianmu*

Though not common in gardens of Suzhou, the Chinese pistache has become an important tree in gardens of Southern California, prized for its beautiful display of fall color. In Liu Fang Yuan, the pistache trees make up part of the deciduous woodland west of the lake. The related *Pistacia vera*, native to western Asia, is heavily cultivated in California's Central Valley for its annual crop of pistachio nuts.

MOCK ORANGE, PITTOSPORUM

海桐 *haitong*

Southern California gardeners will readily recognize pittosporum, native to East Asia, as a common foundation and hedging shrub. Its glossy evergreen foliage is welcome in both shady and sunny areas. A range of forms is available to the gardener, from large and open to dense and compact, and to selections with variegated foliage. Pittosporum brings the bonus of late-spring clusters of fragrant flowers, which is the reason it is sometimes called mock orange.

Pittosporum tobira

PODOCARPUS

羅漢松 *luohansong*

Though not a true pine, the luohan is a true conifer, and not a flowering plant. Flattened evergreen leaves cluster on short stems along the main branches, giving a distinctive tufted character to the foliage. Many different kinds of podocarpus, from subtropical regions around the world, are cultivated in Southern California—with the luohan from southern China and Japan being one of the more frequently seen.

Podocarpus macrophyllus

FLOWERING APRICOT

梅花 *meihua*

Said to be the earliest of the flowering fruit trees, *meihua* comes into full bloom in January, its blossoms resilient to even the coldest frost. The oldest, simple forms have pink or white five-petaled flowers that give us the important plum blossom motif, said to symbolize the five blessings. An unnamed single pink selection at the east entrance to the garden is especially fragrant. Fuller, double forms, like the pink cultivar called 'Peggy Clarke,' are common in Southern California gardens. Plum sauce can be made from the fruit.

Prunus mume

PEACH

桃 *tao*

The emblem of spring, peach trees flower before their leaves unfurl. All peaches make flowers, but the especially showy ones, in colors from white to magenta, are called "flowering peaches" because they are grown for flowers alone and do not produce edible fruit. In summer, peaches are distinguished from the related cherries, plums, and apricots by their long narrow leaves. They are planted throughout Liu Fang Yuan, and are especially important along the Flower Washing Brook and to the east of the brook, where they form a small orchard.

Prunus persica

POMEGRANATE

石榴 *shiliu*

No other plant can be confused with the pomegranate, its fruit a pregnant, leathery purse bursting with seeds, each of which has a tasty, juicy pink coating. Native from the Mediterranean to Southwestern Asia, the pomegranate proved its usefulness and transportability through its ancient adoption by Chinese gardeners.

Punica granatum

OAK

櫟屬 *xiangshu*

Oaks, in general, are one of the great tree groups that characterize the North Temperate flora, with hundreds of species native to areas throughout the Northern Hemisphere. California has its own suite of important oaks, as do most regions of China. Near the Terrace of the Jade Mirror is a young tree of China's *Quercus acutissima*, but most prominent in the garden are numerous ancient specimens of our beautiful native coast live oak, *Q. agrifolia*. Visitors can distinguish the coast live oak by its medium to small dark green and shiny leaves, whose cupped edges have occasional holly-like spines.

Quercus spp.

AZALEA, RHODODENDRON

杜鵑 *dujuan*

Among the most significant contributions to temperate zone horticulture, azaleas and other kinds of rhododendrons from Asia are recognized and appreciated by every gardener. Many deciduous kinds are available, but most garden varieties are low, mounding, evergreen shrubs that flower in a spring flush. They are often planted with camellias, which like azaleas appreciate shade, moisture, and highly organic, acidic soils.

Rhododendron spp.

SACRED LILY

萬年青 *wannianqing*

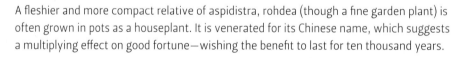

A fleshier and more compact relative of aspidistra, rohdea (though a fine garden plant) is often grown in pots as a houseplant. It is venerated for its Chinese name, which suggests a multiplying effect on good fortune—wishing the benefit to last for ten thousand years.

Rohdea japonica

Salix babylonica

WEEPING WILLOW

垂柳 *chuiliu*

Willows prosper near water, so are commonly planted at the edges of streams and lakes. Alternating with peaches, they are a famed aspect of the West Lake causeway in Hangzhou. In early fall their small fruit open, releasing a drift of snow-like fuzzy seed in what is known as willow blow.

Sapium sebiferum

CHINESE TALLOW TREE

烏桕 *wujiu*

A beautiful relative of the tung oil tree, tallow tree was anciently used for the wax that coats the three white seeds that develop in each fruiting pod. In autumn, the white seed contrast strikingly with the beautiful orange-red autumn color of the leaves, which flex on their elongated stalks with the breeze. Two handsome specimens grow near the lake, standing above the tearoom patio.

Sequoia sempervirens

SEQUOIA, COAST REDWOOD

加州紅木 *jiazhou hongmu*

All Californians should recognize our native coast redwood, a handsome, evergreen conifer that is completely at home with its near relative, China's dawn redwood, *Metasequoia glyptostroboides*, in the cool draw of the valley that embraces the garden. A small grove at the north end of the Flower Washing Brook creates its own garden room of red-brown furrowed and fibrous columns.

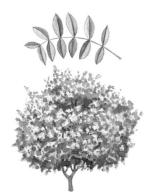

Sophora japonica

CHINESE SCHOLAR TREE

槐樹 *huaishu*

A deciduous tree of modest size, the Chinese scholar tree has long been planted in private gardens and temples as well as along roads and paths in China, where it is associated with the autumn moon and the timing of examinations. The divided leaves give a ferny character to its foliage, and the trunk acquires furrowed bark and wizened branching with age. A scholar tree is planted just south of the Love for the Lotus Pavilion.

CHUSAN PALM, CHINESE WINDMILL PALM

棕櫚 *zonglü*

Native to China, the windmill palm can be encountered in gardens throughout the country. Because it is one of the more cold-hardy palms, it has also become popular around the world for its capacity to bring an exotic, tropical appearance to a temperate garden. The bases of its windmill-like leaves produce coarse fiber, which make the trunks look as though they are wrapped in burlap. These fibers have long been used in China to manufacture rope, coarse cloth, and even brushes.

Trachycarpus fortunei

CHINESE ELM

榔榆 *langyu*

With its small foliage, beautiful branching, and white, rust-flecked trunk, Chinese elm is a lacy and elegant tree. It is also strong and resilient in a dry climate, and has thus become a favorite street and garden tree in Southern California. For these reasons, it was one of Mr. Huntington's favorite trees, and he requested that it be planted near the mausoleum. In autumn, leaves of Chinese elm turn a range of yellow to brown, falling to reveal a handsome architecture.

Ulmus parvifolia

CHINESE WISTERIA

紫藤 *ziteng*

Chinese wisteria, prized for its color and fragrance, is present in most Chinese gardens, climbing over rockwork and up any scaffolding tree or frame. Wisteria flowers, looked at closely, resemble all other pea flowers, with an upright petal called a standard and two petals projecting forward to make a keel. Inside the keel is a small pistil that will grow to become the fruit, a fuzzy bean pod that bursts open with the first winter rains and propels its seed twenty to thirty feet away.

Wisteria sinensis

MAP OF LIU FANG YUAN

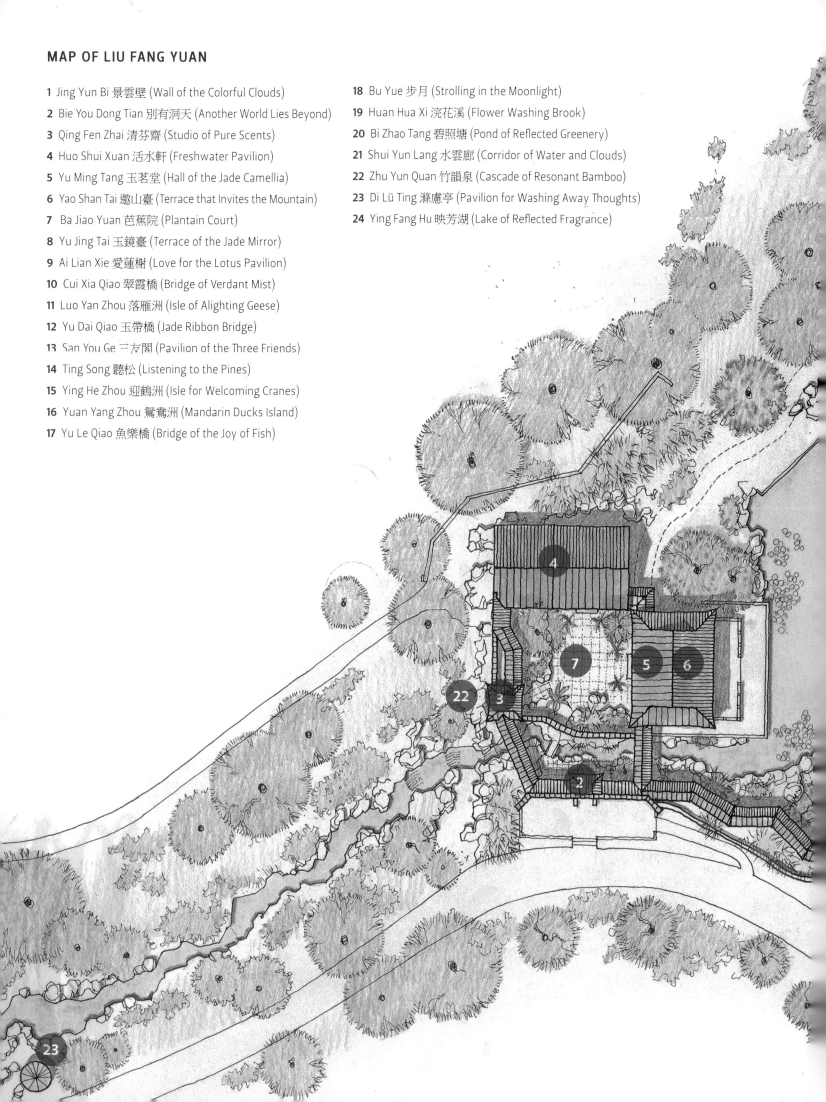

1 Jing Yun Bi 景雲壁 (Wall of the Colorful Clouds)

2 Bie You Dong Tian 別有洞天 (Another World Lies Beyond)

3 Qing Fen Zhai 清芬齋 (Studio of Pure Scents)

4 Huo Shui Xuan 活水軒 (Freshwater Pavilion)

5 Yu Ming Tang 玉茗堂 (Hall of the Jade Camellia)

6 Yao Shan Tai 邀山臺 (Terrace that Invites the Mountain)

7 Ba Jiao Yuan 芭蕉院 (Plantain Court)

8 Yu Jing Tai 玉鏡臺 (Terrace of the Jade Mirror)

9 Ai Lian Xie 愛蓮榭 (Love for the Lotus Pavilion)

10 Cui Xia Qiao 翠霞橋 (Bridge of Verdant Mist)

11 Luo Yan Zhou 落雁洲 (Isle of Alighting Geese)

12 Yu Dai Qiao 玉帶橋 (Jade Ribbon Bridge)

13 San You Ge 三友閣 (Pavilion of the Three Friends)

14 Ting Song 聽松 (Listening to the Pines)

15 Ying He Zhou 迎鶴洲 (Isle for Welcoming Cranes)

16 Yuan Yang Zhou 鴛鴦洲 (Mandarin Ducks Island)

17 Yu Le Qiao 魚樂橋 (Bridge of the Joy of Fish)

18 Bu Yue 步月 (Strolling in the Moonlight)

19 Huan Hua Xi 浣花溪 (Flower Washing Brook)

20 Bi Zhao Tang 碧照塘 (Pond of Reflected Greenery)

21 Shui Yun Lang 水雲廊 (Corridor of Water and Clouds)

22 Zhu Yun Quan 竹韻泉 (Cascade of Resonant Bamboo)

23 Di Lü Ting 滌慮亭 (Pavilion for Washing Away Thoughts)

24 Ying Fang Hu 映芳湖 (Lake of Reflected Fragrance)

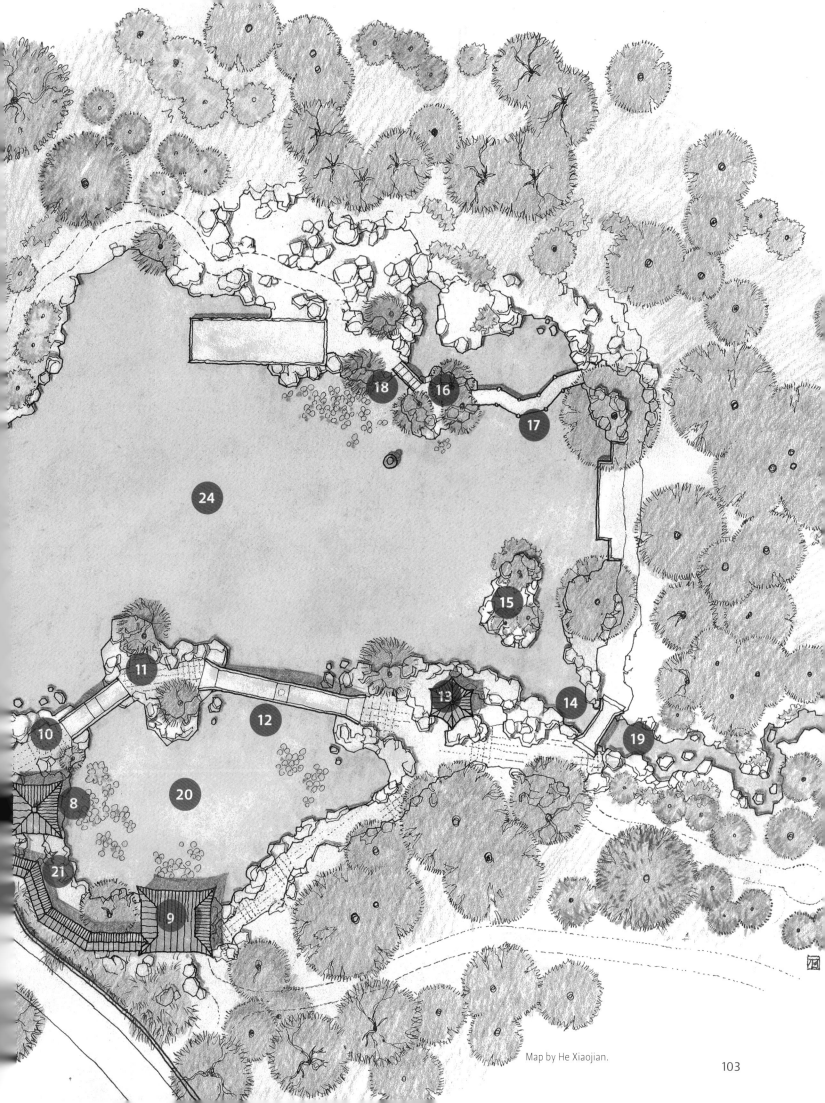

Map by He Xiaojian.

APPENDIX A: NAMES IN LIU FANG YUAN

The numbers correspond to the map on the previous page. Horizontal inscriptions are read from right to left. The original calligraphy is shown here.

1. Jing Yun Bi 景雲壁 (Wall of the Colorful Clouds)

Calligraphy: written by Chen Wei-teh in clerical script; carved brick with charcoal

Reference:
Jingyun 景雲 are brightly colored clouds, regarded as a harbinger of good fortune and associated with royalty. Clouds are also the abode of dragons, aquatic and celestial creatures that provide rain and moisture to nourish the land.

Liu Fang Yuan 流芳園 (Garden of Flowing Fragrance)

Calligraphy: written by Wan-go H. C. Weng in clerical script; carved brick with charcoal

This name reflects the sensory delight of botanical aromas that permeate the Chinese Garden. Their fragrance not only infuses the site but lingers as well—"liu" 流 (flow) puns on "liu" 留 (linger).

References:
  i. This phrase was first used in the poem "Rhapsody on the Luo River Goddess" ("Luoshen fu" 洛神賦), in which the poet Cao Zhi 曹植 (192–232) recounts his romantic encounter with the beautiful goddess of the Luo River. He wrote that she was "sinuous as a swimming dragon," glowing "like a lotus," and moving "lightly like a startled swan." When she moved, he noted that "she treads in the strong pungency of pepper-plant paths / Walks through clumps of scented flora, allowing their fragrance to flow" (踐椒塗之郁烈 / 步蘅薄而流芳). The goddess could only return the poet's longing with glances of her own, since men and gods must remain apart. Soon, she vanished.[1]
  ii. *Liu fang* 流芳 is also the name of Ming dynasty painter Li Liufang 李流芳 (1575–1629).

2. Bie You Dong Tian 別有洞天 (Another World Lies Beyond)

Calligraphy: written by Lo Ching in a combination of seal and clerical scripts; carved wood plaque with pigment

Dongtian 洞天 is "celestial cave," the threshold that leads to paradise.

Reference:
This phrase is from "An Account of Peach Blossom Spring" ("Taohuayuan ji" 桃花源記) by poet Tao Yuanming 陶淵明 (365–427), who recounts a story from his own time. A fisherman follows a bank of blossoming peach trees along a spring and comes upon a small mountain cave. This turns out to be a "celestial cave"; after entering, he discovers an idyllic land where everyone lives in harmony. When he finally returns home, the fisherman cannot find the peach blossom trees again or the perfect world beyond.[2]

---

1. Cao Zhi 曹植, "Luoshen fu" 洛神賦, *Cao Zijian ji* 曹子建集, *Siku quanshu* 四庫全書 ed., 3.1–4.
2. Tao Qian 陶潛, "Taohuayuan ji" 桃花源記, *Tao Yuanming ji* 陶淵明集, *Siku quanshu* ed., 5.1–2.

3. Qing Fen Zhai 清芬齋 (Studio of Pure Scents)

Calligraphy: written by Chen Wei-teh in seal script; carved wood plaque with charcoal

Reference:
The phrase *qing fen* 清芬, meaning "pure scents" or "pure fragrance," is frequently used in classical Chinese poetry. It is also an analogy for "noble virtues," as in these lines of poetry: He sings of the great achievements attained by generations of virtue / And declaims on the pure fragrance of his forbears (詠世德之駿烈 / 誦先人之清芬).[3]

4. Huo Shui Xuan 活水軒 (Freshwater Pavilion)

Calligraphy: written by Yang Ye in semi-cursive script; carved wood plaque with charcoal

Couplet in front of the entrance: written by Yang Ye in semi-cursive script; carved wood plaques with charcoal
小石冷泉留早味 / 紫泥新品泛春華
丁亥夏六月　葉揚書梅聖俞茶詩聯

Translation:
The morning flavor lingers in the cold spring water issuing from the small rocks / Spring blossoms waft from the new tea steeped in a clay teapot
Summer, sixth month of the Dinghai year, Ye Yang wrote Mei Shengyu's[4] *Tea Poem* couplet

Reference:
The name of the tea shop is inspired by the term *huo shui*, which may be rendered more literally as "living water" or "water with a life." It is from a poem on tea by the great scholar Su Dongpo 蘇東坡 (1037–1101). In the poem, Su Dongpo describes how he scoops up the crystal clear "living water" from the deep river in order to make some tea right there on the spot, using a stove where a "living fire," or *huo huo* 活火, is blazing.[5]

Camellia patterns on the six-paneled entrance doorway: design by Liang Peifang 梁北方; carved wood by Suzhou wood carvers; six kinds of camellias, from right to left:
Camellia sasanqua 'Akebono'
Camellia japonica 'Kurume-genji'
Camellia hiemalis 'Kanjirō'
Camellia japonica 'Kōzu'
Camellia japonica 'Kinkō'
Camellia oleifera

5. Yu Ming Tang 玉茗堂 (Hall of the Jade Camellia)

Calligraphy: written by Gao Xiang in clerical script; carved wood plaque with charcoal

Couplet on courtyard entrance: written in clerical script by Lo Ching; carved wood plaque with charcoal
入口百憂去 / 一笑大江橫
丁亥夏日　羅青
Translation:
Enter as a hundred cares vanish / Laugh as the great river expands
Summer, Dinghai year, Lo Ching

Couplet on lakeside entrance: written by Bai Qianshen in semi-cursive-standard script; carved wood plaque with charcoal
流水可為琴曲聽 / 好山須作畫圖看
丁亥夏白謙慎書

---

3. The verses are from Lu Ji 陸機, *Rhapsody on Literature* (*Wen fu* 文賦). The English translation here is by David R. Knechtges; see Tong Xiao and David R. Knechtges, *Wen Xuan, or, Selections of Refined Literature* (Princeton, N.J.: Princeton University Press, 1996), 213.
4. Also known as Mei Yaochen 梅堯臣, 1002–1060.
5. The verse, "Living water should be cooked with living fire" 活水還須活火烹, is from Su Dongpo's poem "Scooping Water from the River to Make Tea" 汲江煎茶. The English translation is from Robert Payne, ed., *The White Pony: An Anthology of Chinese Poetry* (New York: Mentor Books, 1960), 269.

Translation:
The flowing water can be listened to like music from a zither / The fine mountain should be seen as an image in a painting
Summer, Dinghai year, Bai Qianshen wrote this

Reference:
Yu Ming Tang is the name of the residence of playwright Tang Xianzu 湯顯祖 (1550–1616), author of the acclaimed *Peony Pavilion* (*Mudanting* 牡丹亭). The *yuming* 玉茗 flower was an exquisite white camellia. It represented nobility and purity, and was sought after in the eleventh to twelfth centuries, during the Song dynasty. Since camellias belong to the same genus as the tea plant, they form the major motif in the tea house, Yu Ming Tang, and the tea shop, Huo Shui Xuan.

6. Yao Shan Tai 邀山臺 (Terrace that Invites the Mountain)

Calligraphy: written by Terry Yuan in semi-cursive script; engraved Tai Hu rock with pigment

The terrace offers a splendid prospect looking north, borrowing the scenic majesty of the San Gabriel Mountains as a distant view.

7. Ba Jiao Yuan 芭蕉院 (Plantain Court)

Calligraphy: written by Yu Peizhi in seal script; carved brick with pigment

Reference:
The banana plant is identified with the scholar in Chinese art and literature, frequently with references to the sound of raindrops on the broad leaves. The sound evokes a mood of solitude, or even melancholy. The presence of the banana, or plantain, in this courtyard evokes the Chinese scholar, whose taste inspired the style of Liu Fang Yuan.

8. Yu Jing Tai 玉鏡臺 (Terrace of the Jade Mirror)

Exterior Calligraphy: written by Wang Mingfeng in seal script; carved brick

Interior Calligraphy: written by Bai Qianshen in semi-cursive-standard script; carved wood plaque with mineral pigment

Reference:
Yujing 玉鏡, or "jade mirror," is a metaphor for the moon in literature and poetry—a jade-white, round reflection in the heavens. The circular doors on all four sides of this pavilion also emphasize the relationship with the moon. A *tai* 臺 is a "holder," "table," or "terrace," and *yujingtai* 玉鏡臺 literally means "a jade-mirror set," often representing an engagement gift in literature.

9. Ai Lian Xie 愛蓮榭 (Love for the Lotus Pavilion)

Calligraphy: written by Wang Shixiang in standard script; carved wood plaque with charcoal

Couplets on lakeside: written by Lo Ching in a combination of seal and clerical scripts; carved wood plaque with charcoal pigment
污泥豈能染 / 香淡遠益清
二OO七年夏日於大希堂中 羅青

Translation:
Though rooted in the mud, how could the lotus be sullied? / Its subtle fragrance spreads far with even greater purity.
Summer, 2007, in Daxi Studio, Lo Ching

Reference:
The pavilion's name was inspired by a short essay, "Love for the Lotus" ("Ai lian shuo" 愛蓮說), by the distinguished neo-Confucian philosopher Zhou Dunyi 周敦頤 (1017–1073). Expressing himself through the language of flowers, he professes his love for the lotus above all flowers because its pure and perfect blossoms arise above the muddy lakebed, its subtle fragrance spreading out. Zhou Dunyi preferred its understated beauty to that of the lush peony, a fashionable flower cultivated by families of wealth and power during Zhou's time.[6]

10. Cui Xia Qiao 翠霞橋 (Bridge of Verdant Mist)

Calligraphy: written by Liu Ponong in clerical script; carved granite with pigment

Reference:
"Verdant mist" is a poetic reference to lotus leaves hovering just above the water mist. This small bridge overlooks the Pond of Reflected Greenery.

11. Luo Yan Zhou 落雁洲 (Isle of Alighting Geese)

Calligraphy: written by David Hsu in cursive script; carved Tai Hu rock with pigment

Reference:
The image of the graceful descent of migratory wild geese has inspired much art and poetry in China. Their seasonal return suggests human faithfulness. Paired geese are legendary for their romantic devotion and loyalty. Their ability to soar also represents a freedom beyond human reach.

12. Yu Dai Qiao 玉帶橋 (Jade Ribbon Bridge)

Calligraphy: written by Liu Ponong in seal script; carved granite with pigment

Reference:
Jade belts were made of plaques of jade, the most treasured stone in China, sewn onto a belt of gold or other precious material. They were awarded only to the highest-ranking officials by the emperor and thus represent the pinnacle of success in a scholar-official's career.

---

6. Zhou Dunyi 周敦頤, "Ai lian shuo" 愛蓮說, collected in Zhou Shenke 周沈珂, ed., *Zhou Yuangong ji* 周元公集. *Siku quanshu* ed., 2.1–2.

13. San You Ge 三友閣 (Pavilion of the Three Friends)

Calligraphy: written by Terry Yuan in semi-cursive script; carved wood plaque with crushed sand

Reference:
The "three friends of the cold season" are pine, bamboo, and plum. While pine and bamboo stay green throughout the winter, the plum blossoms in early spring when the last frost lingers. Because of their ability to withstand the cold, these three plants have long been identified in Chinese literature and art as symbols of unity, courage, and tenacity.

14. Ting Song 聽松 (Listening to the Pines)

Calligraphy: written by Lo Ching in seal script; carved Tai Hu rock with pigment

Reference:
This name for the small bridge near a long-established stand of pines at the Huntington uses a popular poetic device of evoking sound from, and dialogue with, nature.

15. Ying He Zhou 迎鶴洲 (Isle for Welcoming Cranes)

Calligraphy: written by David Hsu in cursive script; carved Tai Hu rock with pigment

Reference:
The crane has long been associated with longevity in China because it has a long life span, and its white feathers represent old age. It is also identified with the legendary Daoist Immortals.

16. Yuan Yang Zhou 鴛鴦洲 (Mandarin Ducks Island)

Calligraphy: written by David Hsu in cursive script; carved Tai Hu rock with pigment

Reference:
Mandarin ducks are believed to mate for life, and they symbolize a loving and harmonious marriage. They often appear in Chinese literature and art to represent loyal and affectionate couples.

17. Yu Le Qiao 魚樂橋 (Bridge of the Joy of Fish)

Calligraphy: written by Lo Ching in seal script, carved Tai Hu rock with pigment

Reference:

The famous discussion about the joy of fish is found in the Daoist text *Zhuangzi* 莊子, the teachings of master Zhuang, or Zhuang Zhou 莊周 (ca. 369–286 B.C.E.):

Zhuangzi and Huizi 惠子 (ca. 370–310 B.C.E.) were strolling one day on the bridge over the River Hao, when the former observed, "See how the minnows are darting about! Such is the pleasure that fish enjoy." "You are not a fish," said Huizi, "How do you know what fish enjoy?" "You are not I," retorted Zhuangzi, "so how do you know that I do not know what fish enjoy?" "I am not you," said Huizi, "and you are not a fish, and so it is certain that you do not know what fish enjoy." "Let us go back," said Zhuangzi, "to your original question. You asked me *how* I know what fish enjoy. The way you put the question shows that you already knew what I knew. I know that just as we stand here over the Hao." Huizi was a close friend of Zhuangzi. He was also a follower of the Logician school, which was made up of scholars interested in logic and debate. Here we see Zhuangzi using the Daoist idea of relativity to defeat Huizi's logical argument. This selection also shows the playful nature of the stories in *Zhuangzi*.[7]

18. Bu Yue 步月 (Strolling in the Moonlight)

Calligraphy: written by Lo Ching in semi-cursive script; carved granite with pigment

Reference:

The name of this small bridge evokes a poem by the Song dynasty poet Su Dongpo. On a late November night Su Dongpo was wakened by the moonlight coming through his doorway. He went to see his friend at the Temple That Receives the Heavenly (Chengtiansi 承天寺), and together they delighted in the full moonlight of the courtyard. The ground appeared transformed into the surface of water, and the shadows of bamboo and junipers into "aquatic grasses." In the moment they shared, it seemed that no evening was without such a moon, and no place without bamboo and junipers.[8]

19. Huan Hua Xi 浣花溪 (Flower Washing Brook)

Calligraphy: written by David Hsu in cursive script; carved Tai Hu rock with pigment

Reference:

This name is inspired by the Flower-Washing Cottage (Huanhua Caotang 浣花草堂) of Du Fu 杜甫 (712–770),

7. From *Sources of Chinese Tradition*, vol. 1, trans. and ed. William Theodore de Bary et al. (New York: Columbia University Press, 1960). Zhuang Zhou 莊周, "Autumn Flood" 秋水, in Guo Xiang 郭象, ed., *Zhuangzi zhu* 莊子注, *Siku quanshu* ed., 6.19–20.
8. Su Shi's "An Evening Stroll to the Temple That Receives the Heavenly" 記承天夜遊 was written in exile and published posthumously in 1083. See Yang Ye's essay in this volume. For an English translation, see Richard E. Strassberg, *Inscribed Landscapes: Travel Writing from Imperial China* (Berkeley, Calif.: University of California Press, 1994), 192–93. For the Chinese text, see Kong Fanli 孔凡禮, ed., *Su Shi wenji* 蘇軾文集, 6 vols. (Beijing: Zhonghua shuju, 1986), 5:71.2260.

the pre-eminent poet of the Tang dynasty. His cottage was situated by a winding stream that carried along the floating flower petals of late spring. The Late Ming poet Zhong Xing 鍾惺 (1574–1624) remembered this stream as the Flower-Washing Brook in his mini-essay.[9]

Allusions:

    i. Tao Yuanming, "Peach Blossom Spring"[10]

    ii. Wang Xizhi 王羲之 (303–361), "Preface to the Poems Composed at the Orchid Pavilion" ("Lantingji xu" 蘭亭集序). A group of scholars and friends gathered in 353 at the Orchid Pavilion to celebrate the spring purification ceremonies. The great calligrapher Wang Xizhi assembled the poems written that day and attached his famous preface. In a place of mountains and lush forests, he recorded that guests floated their cups down a winding stream. The wine and simple song sufficed to free the "most hidden feelings." Wang's preface became the most sought-after piece of calligraphy for the centuries following.[11]

20. Bi Zhao Tang 碧照塘 (Pond of Reflected Greenery)

Calligraphy: written by David Hsu in cursive script; carved Tai Hu rock with pigment

Reference:
Bi 碧 is a term for jade with emerald tones. This word is often used in poems to describe the greenish or bluish color of water. In Liu Fang Yuan, this small, sectioned-off pond is full of lotus, and the water reflects the shades of green of the lotus leaves.

21. Shui Yun Lang 水雲廊 (Corridor of Water and Clouds)

Calligraphy: written by Lo Ching in seal script; carved wood plaque with pigment

Reference:
Shui 水 (water) and *yun* 雲 (cloud) suggest moisture and mist, which create the most beautiful and poetic landscapes, especially in Southern Chinese gardens. Many paintings, poems, and even musical compositions have depicted such tranquil moisture-laden scenes. A popular *qin*-zither masterpiece is "Mists and Clouds over the Xiao and Xiang Rivers" (*Xiao Xiang shui yun* 瀟湘水雲), composed in the twelfth century.

22. Zhu Yun Quan 竹韻泉 (Cascade of Resonant Bamboo)

Calligraphy: written by Yu Peizhi in clerical script; carved Tai Hu rock with pigment

Reference:
Yun 韻 describes a charming and agreeable sound, as in the tones of poetic rhyme. Here, the rustling of bamboo leaves is harmoniously resonant with the sound of water cascading over the rocks.

---

9. See the essay by Yang Ye in this volume.
10. See item no. 2 above, Bie You Dong Tian (Another World Lies Beyond).
11. See *Jin shu* 晉書, *Siku quanshu* ed., 80.8–9.

24. Ying Fang Hu 映芳湖 (Lake of Reflected Fragrance)

Calligraphy: written by Terry Yuan in semi-cursive script; carved Tai Hu rock with pigment

The name of the main lake is Ying Fang, which means "reflected fragrance." It echoes the name of the garden Liu Fang, or "flowing fragrance."

23. Di Lü Ting 滌慮亭 (Pavilion for Washing Away Thoughts)

Calligraphy: written by Richard Strassberg in semi-cursive script; carved Tai Hu rock with pigment

Couplets at entrance: composed and written in cursive script by Richard Strassberg; carved wood plaque with pigment
流水可清心 / 芳山宜靜觀
石聽泉

Translation:
Flowing water can purify the mind / Fragrant mountains are good for quiet contemplation
Shi Tingquan, or Rocks listening to the Stream (Richard Strassberg's Chinese name)

Reference:
Historically, thatched-roof cottages were the abodes of scholars, poets, and hermits. The name of this thatched pavilion comes from an essay by Liu Zongyuan 柳宗元 (773–819), who wrote for the official Wu Yuanheng 武元衡 (758–815). In the essay, Wu thanks the emperor for the precious gift of new tea, a rare and prized commodity. The sentiments expressed are those of gratitude for the emperor's attention and heartfelt appreciation for the fragrance and fresh taste of new tea. It is helpful in "washing away thoughts," or *di lü* 滌慮. For an official, this was release indeed from all the cares of office.[12]

Seal of Liu Fang Yuan 流芳園: carved by Gao Xiang in Yuan zhuwen 元朱文, developed during the Yuan dynasty (1272–1368) from the revered seal-carving style of scholar-official Zhao Mengfu 趙孟頫 (1254–1322). This style was greatly influential to many famous sixteenth-century Suzhou literati, including Wen Zhengming 文徵明 (1470–1559). The design of this seal opens the complex space of *liu fang* 流芳 on the right side with the broken lines of the frame, while the left side is dominated by the *yuan* 園 character's own frame. The broken lines enclosing the characters *liu fang yuan* 流芳園 create a sense of aged elegance for the seal of the garden.

---

12. Liu Zongyuan 柳宗元, "Wei Wu zhongcheng xie ci xin cha biao" 為武中丞謝賜新茶表, *Liu Hedong ji* 柳河東集, *Siku quanshu* ed., 2.15–16.

APPENDIX B: WOOD MATERIALS IN GARDEN STRUCTURES

3. Studio of Pure Scents 清芬齋 (Qing Fen Zhai)
Wood frame: China fir
Wood carving component: Camphor
Curved railing: Camphor
Lattice-work: China fir

4. The Freshwater Pavilion 活水軒 (Huo Shui Xuan)
Wood frame: China fir
Wood carving component: Camphor
Wood doors and windows: Nanmu
Lattice-work: China fir

5. Hall of the Jade Camellia 玉茗堂 (Yu Ming Tang)
Roof beam: Kapur
Wood frame: China fir
Wood carving component: Camphor
Wood doors and windows: Nanmu
Lattice-work: China fir
Banisters: Yellow cypress

8. Terrace of the Jade Mirror 玉鏡臺 (Yu Jing Tai)
Wood frame: China fir
Wood carving component: Camphor
Lattice-work: China fir

9. Love for the Lotus Pavilion 愛蓮榭 (Ai Lian Xie)
Wood frame: China fir
Wood carving component: Camphor
Curved railing: Camphor
Lattice-work: China fir
Eight Suzhou garden scenes: Nanmu
Plant-theme carving: Yellow cypress
Interior decorative partition: Gingko

13. Pavilion of the Three Friends 三友閣 (San You Ge)
Wood frame: China fir
Wood carving component: Camphor
Curved railing: Camphor
Lattice-work: China fir

21. Corridor of Water and Clouds 水雲廊
(Shui Yun Lang)
Wood frame: China fir
Wood carving component: Camphor
Curved railing: Camphor
Lattice-work: China fir

23. Pavilion for Washing Away Thoughts 滌慮亭
(Di Lü Ting)
Wood pillars: China fir
Wood frame: Camphor

All rafters: China fir

Types of Wood
Camphor (*Cinnamomum camphora*)
   香樟 *xiang zhang*

China fir (*Cunninghamia lanceolata*)
   杉木 *shan mu*

Kapur (*Dryobalanops aromatica*)
   山樟 *shan zhang*

Nanmu (*Phoebe nanmu*)
   楠木 *nanmu* (滇楠 *dian nan*)

Yellow cypress (*Chamaecyparis nootkatensis*)
   黃扁柏 *huang bian bo*

Bai Qianshen 白謙慎 (b. 1955 in Tianjin), a Fujian native, is an associate professor of Asian art history at Boston University. He has published widely on calligraphy, and his recent works include studies of two important seventeenth-century artist-calligraphers, Fu Shan 傅山 and Bada Shanren 八大山人 (or Zhu Da 朱耷). *Calligraphy*, the most popular journal of calligraphy in China, in 2004 named him one of the top ten calligraphers.

Chen Wei-teh 陳維德 (b. 1944 in Nanping, Fujian Province) is chair of the Department of Chinese Literature and dean of the School of Liberal Arts at Mingdao University in Taiwan. A recipient of the Sun Yat-sen Cultural Foundation Award and the Wu Sanlien Foundation Award, Professor Chen is a renowned calligrapher and teacher. He is a member of the Chinese Calligraphy Association and has published works on calligraphy and ancient Chinese philosophers.

Gao Xiang 高翔 (b. 1973 in Xinjiang Province) holds doctoral degrees in medicine and nutrition and a research post in nutritional epidemiology at Harvard University School of Public Health in Boston. He is a serious student of seal-carving and calligraphy, and since 1994 his works have been selected for several exhibitions at the National Museum of China. In addition to his professional publications on medicine and nutrition, Dr. Gao has written about calligraphy and seal-carving of the past and present.

David Hsu, also known as Hsu Ta-wei 徐大衛 (b. 1938), is a native of Ningbo in Zhejiang Province. He came to the United States in the early 1970s and has practiced family medicine for over thirty years. Dr. Hsu, who now lives in San Marino, California, is an avid practitioner of calligraphy, often holding literary gatherings at his home. He is one of the founders of the Chinese Calligraphy Club in Monterey Park, California, serving as chairman in 1988.

Liang Peifang 梁北方, a native of Maoming, Guangdong, has practiced calligraphy and Chinese brush painting for over fifty years. She was greatly influenced by the works of her godfather (or *yifu* 義父), Zhao Shao'ang 趙少昂 (1905–1998), one of the masters of the Lingnan School, and she has apprenticed under some of China's great art masters. After completing her undergraduate work at Danjiang University in Taiwan, Ms. Liang continued her studies in art and design at New York's Fashion Institute of Technology. Her painting style ranges from traditional Chinese techniques to those of Western inspiration, and her works have been collected and exhibited in the United States, the United Kingdom, China, and Singapore, among other countries. Ms. Liang currently lives in Los Angeles, where she continues to paint and exhibit; she also teaches Chinese brush painting for the Huntington's educational programs.

Liu Ponong 劉伯農 (b. 1935 in Shanghai) specializes in *gongbi hua*, or "fine brushwork painting," and is renowned for his elegant and delicate style, especially in bird and flower painting. Beginning in the 1980s, he resided in Southern California, where he was a highly respected teacher of painting and the history of fine art for more than ten years. Professor Liu now lives and works in Taiwan and Shanghai. His works are exhibited in Taiwan and China.

Lo Ching-che 羅青哲 (b. 1948 in Qingdao), a native of Hunan, is better known as Lo Ching. He is an acclaimed poet, artist, and calligrapher. He heads the English Department and the Tiemei Art Center at Mingdao University in Taiwan; previously, he held a distinguished professorship at National Taiwan Normal University. His award-winning works of poetry have been translated into eleven languages. Professor Lo's paintings and calligraphy are represented in the collections of the British Museum, the Ashmolean Museum in Oxford, the St. Louis Art Museum, the China Art Museum in Beijing, and the Taipei Fine Arts Museum, among others.

Richard Strassberg (b. 1948 in New York City), also known as Shi Tingquan 石聽泉, is a professor of Chinese in the Department of Asian Languages and Cultures at the University of California, Los Angeles, and he serves on the Huntington's advisory committee for the Chinese Garden. He has published widely on Chinese painting, calligraphy, and literature, and in particular on the links between literature and Chinese gardens. He is himself an accomplished painter and calligrapher. Professor Strassberg was a speaker at the Huntington symposium "Styles of Chinese Gardens" (2007), and he has also presented public lectures for the Huntington's series on Chinese gardens.

Wang Mingfeng 汪鳴峰 (b. 1956), also known by his studio name Baiyu 白楡, is a native and resident of Suzhou. He is a celebrated calligrapher and seal-carver, and a member of the Jiangsu Calligraphers Association in China. His works of seal-carving can be seen in the publication *Poetry on Ancient Suzhou Bridges* (2006).

Wang Shixiang 王世襄 (b. 1914 in Beijing), a resident of Beijing, has held several key curatorial positions at the Palace Museum. His groundbreaking work *Classic Chinese Furniture: Ming and Early Qing Dynasties* (1991) is based on over forty years of scholarship. He has also devoted much of his writing to the craft traditions of China, including lacquer and bamboo carving. He is a member of the National Commission for Cultural Relics Identification and the Central Research Institute of Culture and History in China.

Wan-go H. C. Weng, also known as Weng Wan-ge 翁萬戈 (b. 1918 in Shanghai), is from a renowned family in Changshu, Jiangsu Province. He was steeped in classical Chinese education in childhood. Since leaving China in 1938, Mr. Weng has made the United States (New Hampshire) his home. He is a scholar, poet, painter, calligrapher, and author. He was a pioneer in the production of documentary and educational films about Chinese art and culture. Mr. Weng is the great-great-grandson of the eminent Weng Tonghe 翁同龢 (1830–1904), from whom he inherited a significant collection of Chinese painting, calligraphy, and books spanning nine hundred years. His groundbreaking 1968 exhibition at the China Institute in America sparked the initial interest in the study of Chinese gardens. He now serves on the Huntington's advisory committee for the Chinese Garden. Mr. Weng was the keynote lecturer at the opening of the Huntington's first exhibition of Chinese art in 2006, "Chrysanthemums on the Eastern Hedge: Gardens and Plants in Chinese Art," to which he loaned many important paintings from his collection.

Ye Yang 葉揚 (b. 1948 in Shanghai), a native of Tongcheng, Anhui Province, is an associate professor in the Department of Comparative Literature and Foreign Languages at the University of California, Riverside. He teaches comparative studies in Chinese and Western literary theory as well as popular culture. Professor Ye's publications include *Vignettes from the Late Ming* (1999), a translation of essays by well-known literati writers of the seventeenth century. Professor Ye serves on the Huntington's advisory committee for the Chinese Garden. He has been a speaker at the Huntington symposium "Styles of Chinese Gardens" (2007) and a lecturer for the Huntington public lecture series on the Chinese Garden.

Yu Peizhi 于培智 (b. 1934 in Shandong Province) is a calligrapher specializing in ancient Chinese scripts. Before coming to California in the 1990s, he devoted many years of study to the inscriptions on Chinese oracle bones and bronze vessels. In 1996, he won the Gold Medal in the Second International Calligraphy Contest held in Seoul, South Korea. Professor Yu currently resides in Los Angeles and travels to China to promote cultural activities in his hometown of Dalian, Liaoning Province.

Terry Yuan (b. 1954 in Shanghai), also known as Yuan Zhizhong 袁志鍾, teaches Chinese calligraphy in the Los Angeles area and serves as advisor for the Chinese Artists Society of the United States. He is also consulting editor for the *Biographical Dictionary of Famous Chinese People* 中華人物辭海. He studied painting and calligraphy under the revered master Liu Haisu 劉海粟 (1896–1994). His calligraphic works have been exhibited in the United States and Asia, including China, Korea, Japan, and Taiwan. He lives in Arcadia, California, with his family.

SELECTED BIBLIOGRAPHY

References in English

Barnhart, Richard M. *Peach Blossom Spring: Gardens and Flowers in Chinese Paintings*. New York: Metropolitan Museum of Art, 1983.

Bickford, Maggie. *Bones of Jade, Soul of Ice: The Flowering Plum in Chinese Art*. New Haven, Conn.: Yale University Art Gallery, 1985.

Brown, Claudia. "Where Immortals Dwell: Shared Symbolism in Painting and Scholars' Rocks."*Oriental Art* 44, no. 1 (Spring 1998): 11–17.

Cahill, James. *The Lyric Journey: Poetic Painting in China and Japan*. Cambridge, Mass.: Harvard University Press, 1996.

Cao Xueqin. *The Story of the Stone*. Translated by David Hawkes. Vol. 1, *The Golden Days*. Harmondsworth, U.K.: Penguin Books, 1973.

Chen Lixian. *Art and Architecture in Suzhou Gardens*. Nanjing, China: Yilin Press, 1992.

Cheng Liyao. *Private Gardens*. Translated by Zhang Long. Ancient Chinese Architecture. New York: Springer-Verlag, 1999.

Chiu Che Bing and Gilles Baud Berthier. *Yuanming Yuan: Le Jardin de la Clarté Parfaite*. Paris: Les Éditions de l'Imprimeur, 2000.

Chung Wah Nan. *The Art of Chinese Gardens*. Hong Kong: Hong Kong University Press, 1982.

Clunas, Craig. *Fruitful Sites: Garden Culture in Ming Dynasty China*. Envisioning Asia. London: Reaktion Books, 1996.

——. "The Gift and the Garden." *Orientations* 26, no. 2 (February 1995): 38–45.

——. "Ideal and Reality in the Ming Garden." In *The Authentic Garden: A Symposium on Gardens*, edited by L. Tjon Sie Fat and E. de Jong, 197–205. Leiden, Netherlands: Clusius Foundation, 1991.

——. *Pictures and Visuality in Early Modern China*. Princeton, N.J.: Princeton University Press, 1997.

——. *Superfluous Things: Material Culture and Social Status in Early Modern China*. Urbana: University of Illinois Press, 1991.

Finnane, Antonia. *Speaking of Yangzhou: A Chinese City, 1550–1850*. Cambridge, Mass.: Harvard University Asia Center, 2004.

Forêt, Phillipe. *Mapping Chengde: The Qing Landscape Enterprise*. Honolulu: University of Hawaii Press, 2000.

Guo Qinghua. *A Visual Dictionary of Chinese Architecture*. Victoria, Australia: Images Publishing, 2002.

Handler, Sarah. *Ming Furniture in the Light of Chinese Architecture*. Berkeley, Calif.: Ten Speed Press, 2005.

Harrist, Robert E., Jr. "Art and Identity in the Northern Song Dynasty: Evidence from Gardens." In *Arts of the Sung and Yüan*, edited by Maxwell K. Hearn and Judith G. Smith, 147–64. New York: Metropolitan Museum of Art, 1996.

——. "Site Names and Their Meanings in the Garden of Solitary Enjoyment." *Journal of Garden History* 13, no. 4 (October–December 1993): 199–202.

Hay, John. *Kernels of Energy, Bones of Earth: The Rock in Chinese Art*. New York: China House Gallery, 1985.

Hu Dongchu. *The Way of the Virtuous: The Influence of Art and Philosophy on Chinese Garden Design*. Beijing: New World Press, 1991.

Hu Kemin. *Scholars' Rocks in Ancient China: The Suyuan Stone Catalog*. Trumbull, Conn.: Weatherhill, Inc., 2002.

Hu, Philip K. "The Shao Garden of Mi Wanzhong (1570–1628): Revisiting a Late Ming Landscape Through Visual and Literary Sources." *Studies in the History of Gardens and Designed Landscapes* 19, nos. 3–4 (July–December 1999): 314–42.

Ji Cheng. *The Craft of Gardens*. Translated by Alison Hardie. New Haven, Conn.: Yale University Press, 1988.

Johnston, R. Stewart. *Scholar Gardens of China: A Study and Analysis of the Spatial Design of the Chinese Private Garden*. Cambridge: Cambridge University Press, 1991.

Keswick, Maggie. *The Chinese Garden*. Cambridge, Mass.: Harvard University Press, 2003.

Knapp, Ronald G. *The Chinese House: Craft, Symbol, and the Folk Tradition*. Hong Kong: Oxford University Press, 1990.

Li Hui-lin. *The Garden Flowers of China*. New York: Ronald Press Co., 1959.

Li, June, and **James Cahill**. *Paintings of Zhi Garden by Zhang Hong: Revisiting a Seventeenth-Century Chinese Garden*. Los Angeles: Los Angeles County Museum of Art, 1996.

Li, T. June. "A Legendary 18th Century Residence: Fang Shishan's Shikan." *Orientations* 36, no. 4 (May 2005): 55–59.

Liang Ssu-ch'eng [Liang Sicheng]. *A Pictorial History of Chinese Architecture: A Study of the Development of Its Structural System and the Evolution of Its Types*. Translated by Wilma Fairbank. Cambridge, Mass.: MIT Press, 1984.

Liu Dunzhen. *Chinese Classical Gardens of Suzhou*. Translated by Joseph C. Wang. New York: McGraw-Hill, 1993.

Makeham, John. "The Confucian Role of Names in Traditional Chinese Gardens." *Studies in the History of Gardens & Designed Landscapes* 18, no. 3 (Autumn 1998): 187–210.

Métailié, Georges. "Insight into Chinese Traditional Botanical Knowledge." In *The Authentic Garden: A Symposium on Gardens*, edited by L. Tjon Sie Fat and E. de Jong, 215–24. Leiden, Netherlands: Clusius Foundation, 1991.

——. "Some Hints on 'Scholar Gardens' and Plants in Traditional China." *Studies in the History of Gardens & Designed Landscapes* 18, no. 3 (Autumn 1998): 248–56.

Meyer-Fong, Tobie. *Building Culture in Early Qing Yangzhou*. Stanford, Calif.: Stanford University Press, 2003.

Munakata, Kiyohiko. "Mysterious Heavens and Chinese Classical Gardens." *RES: Anthropology and Aesthetics* 15 (Spring 1988): 61–88.

Murk, Alfreda, and **Wen Fong**. *A Chinese Garden Court: The Astor Court of the Metropolitan Museum of Art*. New York: Metropolitan Museum of Art, 1980.

Owen, Stephen, ed. and trans. *An Anthology of Chinese Literature: Beginnings to 1911*. New York: W. W. Norton, 1996.

Schafer, Edward H. *Tu Wan's Stone Catalog of Cloudy Forest*. Berkeley, Calif.: University of California Press, 1961.

Sensabaugh, David Ake. "Fragments of Mountain and Chunks of Stone: The Rock in the Chinese Garden." *Oriental Art* 44, no. 1 (Spring 1998): 18–27.

Shen Fu. *Six Records of a Floating Life*. Translated by Leonard Pratt and Chiang Su-hui. London: Penguin Books, 1983.

Silbergeld, Jerome. "Beyond Suzhou: Region and Memory in the Gardens of Sichuan." *The Art Bulletin* 86, no. 2 (June 2004): 207–27.

Smith, Joanna F. Handlin. "Gardens in Ch'i Piao-chia's Social World: Wealth and Values in Late-Ming Kiangnan." *Journal of Asian Studies* 51, no. 1 (February 1992): 58–81.

Steinhardt, Nancy Shatzman, ed. *Chinese Architecture*. New Haven and Beijing: Yale University Press and New World Press, 2002.

Strassberg, Richard E., trans. *Inscribed Landscapes: Travel Writing from Imperial China*. Berkeley, Calif.: University of California Press, 1994.

Stuart, Jan. "Ming Dynasty Gardens Reconstructed in Words and Images." *Journal of Garden History* 10, no. 3 (1990): 162–72.

———. "A Scholar's Garden in Ming China: Dream and Reality." *Asian Art* 3, no. 4 (Fall 1990): 31–51.

Tsu, Francis Ya-sing. *Landscape Design in Chinese Gardens*. New York: McGraw-Hill, 1988.

Valder, Peter. *Gardens in China*. Portland, Ore.: Timber Press, 2002.

———. *The Garden Plants of China*. Sydney: Florilegium, 1999.

Weng, Wan-go H. C. *Gardens in Chinese Art: From Private and Museum Collections*. New York: China Institute in America and China House Gallery, 1968.

Xiao Chi. *The Chinese Garden as Lyric Enclave: A Generic Study of "The Story of the Stone."* Ann Arbor: Center of Chinese Studies, University of Michigan, 2001.

Xu Yinong. "The Traditional Gardens of Suzhou." *Garden History* 10, no. 2 (Autumn 1982): 80–141.

Yang Hongxun. *The Classical Gardens of China: History and Design Techniques*. Translated by Wang Huimin. New York: Van Nostrand Reinhold, 1982.

Yang Xiaoshan. *Metamorphosis of the Private Sphere: Gardens and Objects in Tang-Song Poetry*. Cambridge, Mass.: Harvard University Asia Center, 2003.

Ye Yang. *Vignettes from the Late Ming: A Hsiao-p'in Anthology*. Seattle: University of Washington Press, 1999.

Zeitlin, Judith. "The Secret Life of Rocks: Objects and Collectors in the Ming and Qing Imagination." *Orientations* 30, no. 5 (May 1999): 40–47.

Zhu Junzhen. *Chinese Landscape Gardening*. Beijing: Foreign Languages Press, 1992.

References in Chinese

An Huaiqi 安怀起. *Zhongguo yuanlin shi* 中国园林史 [A history of the Chinese garden]. Shanghai: Tongji daxue chubanshe, 1991.

——. *Zhongguo yuanlin yishu* 中国园林艺术 [The art of the Chinese garden]. Shanghai: Shanghai kexue jishu chubanshe, 1986.

Cao Lindi 曹林娣. *Ninggu de shi: Suzhou yuanlin* 凝固的诗: 苏州园林 [Frozen poetry: the gardens of Suzhou]. Beijing: Zhonghua shuju, 1960.

Cao Minggang 曹明纲. *Renjing hutian: Zhongguo yuanlin wenhua* 人境壶天: 中国园林文化 [World of humans, heaven in a teapot: the culture of the Chinese garden]. Shanghai: Shanghai guji chubanshe, 1994.

Chen Congzhou 陈从周, ed. *Zhongguo yuanlin jianshang cidian* 中国园林鉴赏词典 [A dictionary of Chinese gardens]. Shanghai: Huadong shifan daxue chubanshe, 2001.

——. *Shuo yuan* 说园 [On Chinese gardens]. Shanghai: Tongji daxue chubanshe, 1984.

——. *Yuanlin tancong* 园林谈从 [Collected discussions about Chinese gardens]. Shanghai: Shanghai wenhua chubanshe, 1980.

Chen Zhi 陈植 and Zhang Gongchi 张公驰, eds. *Zhongguo lidai mingyuanji xuanzhu* 中国历代名园记选注 [Selected, Annotated Records of Famous Gardens through History]. Hefei, China: Anhui kexue jishu chubanshe, 1983.

Ding Liangcai 丁良才 and Shanghai Yuyuan guanlichu 上海豫园管理处, eds. *Yuyuan: Fengguang pian* 豫园: 风光篇 [Yuyuan garden: scenes]. 1999.

Jieziyuan huapu 芥子園畫譜 [The Mustard Seed Garden manual of painting]. Taipei: Huazheng shuju 華正書局, 1979.

Peng Yigang 彭一刚. *Zhongguo gudian yuanlin fenxi* 中国古典园林分析 [An analysis of Chinese classical gardens]. Beijing: Zhongguo jianzhu gongye chubanshe, 1986.

Ren Changtai 任常泰 and Meng Ya'nan 孟亚男. *Zhongguo yuanlin shi* 中国园林史 [A history of Chinese gardens]. Beijing: Yanshan chubanshe, 1993.

Shao Zhong 邵忠 and Jin Li 李瑾 eds. *Suzhou lidai mingyuan ji/Suzhou yuanlin chongxiu ji* 苏州历代名园记/苏州园林重修记 [Records of famous gardens in Suzhou through the ages/Records of restorations of Suzhou gardens]. Beijing: Zhongguo linye chubanshe, 2004.

Wang Yi 王毅. *Yuanlin yu Zhongguo wenhua* 园林与中国文化 [Gardens and Chinese culture]. Shanghai: Shanghai renmin chubanshe, 1990.

——. *Zhongguo yuanlin wenhuashi* 中国园林文化史 [A cultural history of Chinese gardens]. Shanghai: Shanghai renmin chubanshe, 2004.

Xu Wentao 徐文涛. *Wangshi yuan* 网师园 [Garden of the Master of Fishnet]. Suzhou, China: Suzhou daxue chubanshe, 1997.

——. *Zhuozheng yuan* 拙政园 [Garden of the Artless Administrator]. Suzhou, China: Suzhou daxue chubanshe, 1998.

Zhang Jiaji 张家骥, ed. *Zhongguo yuanlin yishu dacidian* 中国园林艺术大辞典 [A dictionary of Chinese garden art]. Taiyuan, China: Shanxi jiaoyu chubanshe, 1997.

INDEX

Page numbers in bold refer to illustrations.

Ai Lian Xie (Love for the Lotus Pavilion), **27**, 58, **59**, **66**, **67**, 67, 108, 113
Another World Lies Beyond (Bie You Dong Tian) (Another Heaven Inside the Cave), **56**, 56, 105
apricot, 75, 79, 97
azalea, 24, 77, 78, 98

Ba Jiao Yuan (Plantain Court), **55**, **81**, 107
Bai Qianshen (1955–), 106–7, 114
bamboo, 67, 78, 79, **82**, 84, 86
    three friends of the cold season and, 58, 69, 83, 109
banana, 81, 94, 107
    See also Plantain Court (Ba Jiao Yuan)
banana shrub, 94
Bauhinia blakeana, 81
Bi Zhao Tang (Pond of Reflected Greenery), 67, 108, 111
Bie You Dong Tian (Another World Lies Beyond), **56**, 56, 105
Borthwick, John David (1825–1900), 10
Bridge of the Joy of Fish (Yu Le Qiao), 58, 63, 110
Bridge of Verdant Mist (Cui Xia Qiao), 108
Bu Yue (Strolling in the Moonlight), 58, 110
Buddha's Hand citron, 89
Buddhism, 44, 58, 60–61, 78

calligraphy, **26**, 43, 49, 63, 70, **105–12**
camellia, 24, 70, 76, 78, 82, 87
    C. sinensis, 64, 78, 87
    motif, 64, **64–65**, 67, 106–7
camphor, 37, 88, 113
Cao Zhi (192–232), *Rhapsody on the Luo River Goddess*, 20, 105
carving, 24, 37, 63, 105–13
    stone, 25, 69
    wood, 25, 33, 38, 64, 67, 69, **106**
Cascade of Resonant Bamboo (Zhu Yun Quan), 70, 111
cedar, California incense, 86
Chen Jin, 9, 28, 29
Chen Wei-teh (1944–), 105, 106, 114
cherry, Taiwan, **85**

China fir, 113
Chinese elm, 100
Chinese fringe tree, 88
Chinese Garden. *See* Liu Fang Yuan (Garden of Flowing Fragrance)
Chinese juniper, 92
Chinese parasol tree, 90
Chinese pistache, 96
Chinese privet, 93
Chinese scholar tree, 99
Chinese tallow tree, 99
Chinese windmill palm, **80**, 80, 100
Chinese wisteria, 100
chrysanthemum, 75, 77, 83, 88
    motif, 35, 63, **64**, 67
chusan palm, 100
citrus, 75, 80, 84, 89
    C. sinensis, 75, 80, 84
clerical script, 105, 106, 108, 111
coast redwood, 99
Confucius (551–479 BCE), 44
Corridor of Water and Clouds (Shui Yun Lang), 111, 113
crape myrtle, 83, 92
Cui Xia Qiao (Bridge of Verdant Mist), 108
cursive script, 106–12
cymbidium, 89
cypress, 37, 67, 113

Daoism, 44, 56, 63, 110
dawn redwood, 81, 93
daylily, 77, 91
Desert Garden, Huntington, 23
Di Lü Ting (Pavilion for Washing Away Thoughts), 24, **24**, 70, 112, 113
dogwood, 76, 83
A Dream of Red Mansions. See *The Story of the Stone* (*Shitouji*)
The Dream of the Red Chamber. See *The Story of the Stone* (*Shitouji*)
Du Fu (712–770), 58, 69, 110–11

elm, 82, 83
   Chinese, 100
empress tree, 96

Fan Qi (1616–after 1694), *Peach Blossom Spring*, **57**
Fan Yi (active ca. 1658–71), *Purification at the Orchid Pavilion*, **70–71**
Feng Dayou (twelfth century), *Lotuses in the Wind at T'aiye*, **66**
fir, 37
   China, 113
Firmiana, 80, 90
Flower Washing Brook (Huan Hua Xi), 58, 69, 93, 97, 110
Folsom, James, 8–9, 23, 75–84
forsythia, 75, 83, 90
   F. suspensa, **78**
Freshwater Pavilion (Huo Shui Xuan), 35, **60**, 60–61, 106, 113
   camellia motif in, 64, 67, 106
fringe tree, Chinese, 88
Fry, Jim, 9, 30, **30**

Gao Xiang (1973–), 106, 112, 114
Garden of Flowing Fragrance. *See* Liu Fang Yuan (Garden of Flowing Fragrance)
Garden of Glorious Breezes, 47
Garden of Solitary Delight, 49
gardenia, 78, 84, 90
ginkgo, 23, 37, 80, 83, **83**, 90
golden rain tree, 92
Grand View Garden, 50
Great Wall, **83**
Gu Kaizhi (ca. 345–406), *Goddess of the Luo River*, 20
Guangzhou Province, 81
Guo Zhongshu (917–977), 46

Hall of the Jade Camellia (Yu Ming Tang), **31**, **34**, 64, 106–7, 113
Han dynasty (206 BCE–220 CE), 47
Han palace, **45**
handscrolls, **20**, **21**, **25**, **46–47**, **48**, **70–71**
He Fengchun, 30
He Xiaojian, 103
heavenly bamboo, 94
Hertrich, William (1878–1966), 20, 23
hibiscus, 91
   H. rosa-sinensis, **75**, 91

Hong, Y. C., 12
Hong Kong, 80–81
Hsu, David (1938–), 108, 109, 110, 111, 114
Huan Hua Xi (Flower Washing Brook), 58, 69, 110
Huizi, 63, 110
Huizong (Song-dynasty emperor), 60
Huntington, Henry Edwards (1850–1927), 8, 11, 20, 23, 25
Huntington Library, Chinese historical collections of, 11–12
Huo Shui Xuan (Freshwater Pavilion), 35, **60**, 60–61, 106, 113
   camellia motif in, 64, 67, 106

incense cedar, California, 86
inscriptions, 24, 26, 50, 56, 61, **69**, **105–12**
Isle for Welcoming Cranes (Ying He Zhou), 109
Isle of Alighting Geese (Luo Yan Zhou), 108

Jade Ribbon Bridge (Yu Dai Qiao), **18**, **35**, 108
Japanese Garden, Huntington, 8, **22**, 23, 24, **84**, **85**
jasmine, 78, 84, 91
Ji Cheng (seventeenth century), 26
   The Craft of Gardens, 23–24
Jia Baoyu (literary character), 48, 50, 53, 55
Jia Yuanchun (literary character), 50
Jia Zheng (literary character), 44, 48, 50, 53
Jiangnan region, 24–25, 49, 50
Jin dynasty, 20
Jing Yun Bi (Wall of the Colorful Clouds), **19**, 105
juniper, 78, 83
   Chinese, 92

kapur, 113
kumquat, 80, 89

Lake of Reflected Fragrance (Ying Fang Hu), **19**, 26, **26**, 58, 112
landscape painting, 20, **21**, 26, 61
Leese, Jacob P., 13
Li, T. June, 9, 15, 19–27, 63–70
Li Liufang (1575–1629), 20, 105
   Thin Forest and Distant Mountains, **21**
Liang Peifang, 64–65, 106, 114
lilac, 75, 78, 84
lily, 76, 77
   sacred, 98

lily turf, **82**, 95
Listening to the Pines (Ting Song), 69, **69**, 109
literati, 63, 112, 115
Liu Fang Yuan (Garden of Flowing Fragrance)
   construction, 29–39
   design, 23–26, 31–32, 35
   motifs, 30, 35, 63–64, 67, 69, 106
   naming of, 19–20, 50–51, 53, 55, 105
   origins of, 8–9, 23
   plants, 81–85
   See also specific structures
Liu Ponong (1935–), 108, 114
Liu Zongyuan, 112
Lo Ching (1948–), 105, 106, 108, 109, 110, 111, 115
lotus, 58, **66**, 67, 83, 95, 108, 111
Love for the Lotus Pavilion (Ai Lian Xie), **27**, 58, **59**,
   66, **67**, 67, 108, 113
Lu Hongren, 30
Lu Yu (733–804), *The Classic on Tea*, 60
Luo River goddess, **20**, 20, 105
Luo Yan Zhou (Isle of Alighting Geese), 108
Luoyang, China, 49

magnolia, **74**, 80, 83
   Southern, 81
   yulan, 93
Mandarin Ducks Island (Yuan Yang Zhou), 109
map of Liu Fang Yuan, **102–3**
maple, 23, 80, 83, 84, 86
Marsh, George T., 23
mei hua (*Prunus mume*), 79, 79, 97
   three friends of the cold season and, 58, **68**, 69,
   83, 109
Mei Shengyu, 61
   Tea Poem, 106
Mei Yaochen (1002–1060), 61
   Tea Poem, 106
Mi Wanzhong, 25
Michelia alba, **80**, 80, 84
M. figo, 94
Ming dynasty (1368–1644)
   artists, 20, 21, 25, 46, 48, 105
   gardens, 15, 24, 26, 49
   poets, 58
mock orange, 97
mondo grass, 84, 95

mountains, 24, 26, 69, 70, 107
moutan, 96
mulberry, 80
   white, 94
Mustard Seed Garden Manual of Painting (*Jieziyuan
   Huapu*), 64, **64**

nandina, 78, 82, 94
nanmu, 67, 113
narcissus, 84, 95
North Temperate climate, 76–77, 82

oak, 24, 26, 82, 83, 84, 98
Offenhauser, Bob Ray, 29
Offenhauser and Associates, 30
orange, sweet, 75, 80, 84, 89
orchid, 67
Orchid Pavilion, 69, **70–71**, 111
orchid tree, 81
Oriental Garden, Huntington, 8, **22**, 23
osmanthus
   golden, 84
   O. fragrans, 78, 95
   sweet, 95

Paanakker, Peter, 8
Paeonia suffruticosa 'Qing Lo,' 77
Palace of Everlasting Joy, 47
palm
   Chinese windmill, 80, **80**, 100
   chusan, 100
   sago, 89
Palm Garden, Huntington, **80**
parasol tree, Chinese, 90
Pavilion for Washing Away Thoughts (Di Lü Ting), **24**,
   24, 70, 112, 113
Pavilion of Drenched Blossoms, 48
Pavilion of the Three Friends (San You Ge), 58, **59**, 67,
   68, 69, 109, 113
peach, 75, 78, 79, 83, 85, 97
"Peach Blossom Spring," 56–57, 61, 69, 105, 111
penjing, 77
peony, 75, 77, 83
   tree, 96
persimmon, 80
phoenix tree, 90

pine, 24, 67, 79, 80, 84, 96, 113
    three friends of the cold season and, 58, **68**, 69, 83, 109
pistache, 23, 83
    Chinese, 96
pittosporum, 97
plane tree, 81, **81**
plantain, **81**, 81, 84, 94, 107
Plantain Court (Ba Jiao Yuan), **55**, **81**, 87, 94, 107
Platanus, 81, **81**
plum, 67, 75, 79
    three friends of the cold season and, 58, **68**, 69, 83, 109
podocarpus, **78**, 97
poetry
    court, 47
    for gardens, 24, 49
    gatherings, 69–70
    for Liu Fang Yuan, 105–11
    lyric, 50–51
    Rhapsody on the Luo River Goddess, 20
    on tea, 61
pomegranate, 81, 98
Pond of Reflected Greenery (Bi Zhao Tang), 67, 108, 111
primrose jasmine, 91
princess tree, 96
privet, Chinese, 93
Prospect Garden, 50
Prunus, 24
    P. campanulata, 85
    P. mume, 58, 79, 79, 83, 97, 109
    P. persica, 75, 97
    P. taiwaniana, 85

Qing dynasty (1644–1911), 24, 26, 48, 54, 71
Qing Fen Zhai (Studio of Pure Scents), **40–41**, 70, 85, 106, 113
Qiu Ying (1494–1552), *The Garden for Self-Enjoyment*, **46–47**
quince, 79, 87

redwood, 93
Revere, Joseph Warren (1812–1880), 10
rhododendron, 98
    R. 'Forsterianum,' **76**

rocks. *See* Tai Hu rocks
rose, 75, 76

sago palm, 89
San Gabriel Mountains, 24, 26, 69, 70, 86, 107
San You Ge (Pavilion of the Three Friends), 58, **59**, 67, **68**, 69, 109, 113
scholar tree, 80, 99
seal, 112
seal script, 105–11
sequoia, 99
Shanghai, 78, 81, **81**
Shao Garden, **25**
Shaoxing, China, 69
Shen Guohua (fifteenth century), *Wangchuan Villa*, **46**
Shen Zongqian (1736–1820), 61
Shi Tingquan, 112
Shui Yun Lang (Corridor of Water and Clouds), 111, 113
silk, 94
Sima Guang (1019–1086), "A Record of the Garden of Solitary Delight," 49
Song dynasty (960–1279), 20, 45, 49, 58, 60, 66, 107
Sophora, 80, 99
Sowd, Laurie, 9, 29–39
standard script, 108
The Story of the Stone (*Shitouji*), 44, **49**, 50, 53, **54**, 55
Stowe, England, **44**
Strassberg, Richard (1948–), 19, 43–51, 112, 115, 118
Strolling in the Moonlight (Bu Yue), 58, 110
Studio of Pure Scents (Qing Fen Zhai), **40–41**, 70, 85, 106, 113
Su Dongpo. *See* Su Shi (Su Shih) (1037–1101)
Su Shi (Su Shih) (1037–1101), 51, 60–61, 106, 110
Su the Eastern Slope. *See* Su Shi (Su Shih) (1037–1101)
Sun Wen (nineteenth century), *A Dream of Red Mansions*, 48, 54
sutras, 58
    See also Buddhism
Suzhou
    artisans, 29–32, 38, 64
    garden culture, 15, 25–26, 49, 67
    plants, 81–82
    Taihu rocks and, 39
Suzhou Garden Development Company, 30
Suzhou Institute of Landscape Architecture Design, 9, 30, 32

sweetgum, 83, 93
symbolism, 63
    of lotus, 58, 67, 83
    of plants, 44, 81, 82
    of three friends of the cold season, 69, 109

Tai Hu rocks, 25, 26, **38**, 39, **39**, 107–12
Taiwan, 80
Taiwan cherry, **85**
tallow tree, Chinese, 99
Tang dynasty (618–907), 46, 47, 60, 111
Tang Xianzu (playwright) (1550–1616), *Peony
    Pavilion*, 64, 107
Tao Yuanming (365–427), 63
    "Peach Blossom Spring," 56–57, 61, 69, 105, 111
Taoism. *See* Daoism
tea, 23, 60–61, 64, 67, 78, 87, 106–7, 112
    See also camellia
tea house. *See* Hall of the Jade Camellia (Yu
    Ming Tang)
tea olive, 78, 84, 95
tea shop. *See* Freshwater Pavilion (Huo Shui Xuan)
Terrace of the Jade Mirror (Yu Jing Tai), **27**, 107, 113
Terrace that Invites the Mountain (Yao Shan Tai), 107
thatched-roof pavilion, 24, 58, 70, 112
three friends of the cold season, 58, **68**, 69, 83, 109
Tiger Hill, Suzhou, **77**
tiles, roof, 25, 31, 35–36, 63–64
Ting Song (Listening to the Pines), **69**, 69, 109
Trachycarpus fortunei, **80**, 100
Tsu, Frances, 8, 29

ValleyCrest Landscape Development Company, 9,
    31–32, 38
viburnum, **78**

Wall of the Colorful Clouds (Jing Yun Bi), **19**, 105
Wang Mingfeng (1956–), 107, 115
Wang Shixiang (1914–), 108, 115
Wang Wei (701–761), 46, 47
Wang Xizhi (303–361), "Preface to the Poems
    Composed at the Orchid Pavilion," 70, 111
Wen Zhengming, 112
Weng, Wan-go H. C. (1918–), 15, 19, 25, 105, 115
Western gardens, 43, 75–77

willow, 82, 83, 84
    weeping, 99
windmill palm, Chinese, **80**, 80, 100
wintersweet, 87
wisteria, 75, 84, **84**
    Chinese, 100
Wu Bin (active 1573–1620), *Mi Wanzhong's Shao
    Garden*, **25**
Wu Yuanheng, 112

Xie Huan (ca. 1370–ca. 1450), 48
Xie Lingyun (385–443), 47

Yangzi River, 25, 35, 51
Yao Shan Tai (Terrace that Invites the Mountain), 107
Ye Yang (1948–), 19, 53–61, 106, 115, 118
Ying He Zhou (Isle for Welcoming Cranes), 109
Yu Dai Qiao (Jade Ribbon Bridge), **18**, **35**, 108
Yu Jing Tai (Terrace of the Jade Mirror), **27**, 107, 113
Yu Le Qiao (Bridge of the Joy of Fish), 58, 63, 110
Yu Ming Tang (Hall of the Jade Camellia), **31**, **34**, 64,
    106–7, 113
Yu Peizhi (1934–), 107, 111, 115
Yuan, Terry (1954–), 107, 109, 112, 115
Yuan dynasty, 112
Yuan Yang Zhou (Mandarin Ducks Island), 109
yulan, 93

Zhao Boju, *The Han Palace*, **45**
Zhao Mengfu (1254–1322), 112
Zhao Mengjian (1199–1264), *Three Friends of the Cold
    Season*, **68**
Zhong Xing (1574–1624), 58, 111
Zhou Dunyi (1017–1073), "A Note on the Love of
    Lotus," 58, 67, 108
Zhu Da, 114
Zhu Yun Quan (Cascade of Resonant Bamboo), 70, 111
Zhuangzi, 58, 63, 110

EDITOR'S ACKNOWLEDGMENTS

This book would not have been possible without the careful attention and generous help of many colleagues and friends. Their selfless participation in this project was pivotal to its creation.

First and foremost, I want to thank Peter and Helen Bing for believing in us and providing the funding to make this book a reality.

From the start, both Steven Koblik, President of the Huntington, and Robert C. Ritchie, W. M. Keck Foundation Director of Research, championed our concept of publishing a book to record the extraordinary project of building a Chinese garden. I thank all the authors for their participation and fervent support.

As the fount of botanical information, explanations, and references, David MacLaren, Curator of the Asian Gardens, and Kathy Musial, Curator of the Living Collections and Collection Manager at the Huntington, have been ever generous. I also thank Danielle Rudeen, assistant to the director of the Botanical Gardens, and Cynthia Dickie, administrative assistant, for their willingness to help with any request.

For enhancing the artistic scope of the book, I thank John Sullivan, Senior Photographer at the Huntington, who supplied many striking photographs with enthusiasm and skill; and to Donald Alschuler, a friend to the Chinese Garden, for extensively documenting in photographs the building of the garden from the very beginning. Lisa Pompelli's charming and wonderful illustrations have greatly enriched the plant list. I am also much obliged to Marci Boudreau and Vesna Petrovic of Picnic Design for the pleasing and creative layout of the book.

For their help with bibliographic organization and research, I am very grateful to Han-yun Chang and Kathryn Venturelli, colleagues in the Chinese Garden office, who have gallantly chased down details and systematized information. I thank them for their unconditional support and generous contributions.

The expertise of our editors at the Huntington has been indispensable in sharpening the essays and shaping the book. I am deeply thankful to Susan Green, Director of the Huntington Library Press, and Jean Patterson, Managing Editor, for their inspirational calm and guidance. A final thank you goes to the many other members of the Huntington staff who made essential contributions to the construction of the garden and to the production of this book.

T. June Li, Curator of Liu Fang Yuan
The Chinese Garden at the Huntington
October 2008